How to Avoid Illness and Infection

Also available:

In the Health and Safety in Early Years Settings series:

How to Keep Young Children Safe
Lynn Parker
1-84312-301-0

How to Do a Health and Safety Audit
Lynn Parker
1-84312-303-7

Other:

The A–Z of School Health: A Guide for Teachers
Adrian Brooke and Steve Welton
1-84312-830-4

How to Avoid Illness and Infection

Lynn Parker

David Fulton Publishers

This edition reprinted 2007 by Routledge
2 Park Square, Milton Park, Abingdon, Oxon, OX14 4RN
Simultaneously published in the USA and Canada
by Routledge
270 Madison Avenue, New York, NY 10016

First published in Great Britain in 2006 by David Fulton Publishers

10 9 8 7 6 5 4 3 2 1

British Library Cataloguing in Publication Data
A catalogue record for this book is available from the British Library.

ISBN: 1 84312 299 5

Typeset by FiSH Books, Enfield, Middx.
Printed and bound in Great Britain

Contents

Foreword by Sandy Green   vi

Introduction to the series   vii

Key information   viii
    Calling the emergency services   viii
    How to wash hands effectively   ix
    How to do the meningitis 'tumbler' test   x

Part 1: Illness and Infection   1
  1 Preventing illness and infection   3
  2 Making and keeping a clean environment   22
  3 Safety in the baby room   39
  4 Managing illness   57
  5 Record keeping and administering medicines   81

Part 2: Specific Diseases   91
  6 Signs and symptoms of common communicable diseases 93
  7 Other communicable diseases   100
  8 Contagious conditions of the skin and hair   104

Appendix 1: Useful contact details   107

Appendix 2: Audit tool   110

Appendix 3: Diseases notifiable (to LA Proper Officers) under the Public
         Health (Control of Diseases) Act 1984 and the Public Health
         (Infectious Diseases) Regulations 1988   112

Bibliography   113

Index   115

Foreword

Working with young children is both a pleasure and a privilege, but with each of these comes responsibility. One key area of responsibility is health and safety. Managers of all early years settings need a clear understanding of what is required, both to fulfil their duties and to impart knowledge to their staff and those training with them. These books will help achieve this.

One of the first things students undertaking training in early years are introduced to is safe practice, both for themselves and for the children they will work with. The importance of taking responsibility for personal safety is discussed in this series along with how to observe and supervise children appropriately. The *Health and Safety in the Early Years* series presents three accessible books covering all the main aspects of health and safety in early years environments under three main topics. These books will be of considerable use to managers, qualified practitioners and students on a range of courses.

The series can be read as a set, perhaps to support assignment work or within staff training, or as stand-alone texts. Managers will find examples to help them support the development of their staff, as the books present information that will both consolidate and extend understanding for most readers. Useful chapter summaries and best-practice checklists help give an 'at-a-glance' reminder of what should be happening today and every day. The use of bullet points for emphasis throughout the books works well, and each book includes a comprehensive list of references and/or contacts.

In *How to Avoid Illness and Infection* the emphasis is partly on prevention, through cleanliness and good hygiene, and partly on managing illness, including details of communicable illnesses. Clear, practical guidelines are given, e.g. teaching children to wash their hands thoroughly, a common source of cross-infection.

This series highlights why revisiting understanding and updating knowledge of this area of responsibility are so important.

Sandy Green – Early Years Consultant
January 2006

Introduction to the series

This book is one of a series of three addressing the issue of health and safety within the early years setting. Those who work with young children have a responsibility for providing a safe environment to ensure their well-being. The National Standards provide a baseline for the provision of quality child care but you also need to comply with national legislation covering health and safety, food hygiene and fire safety.

This book considers the factors that influence the spread of infection relating to children, along with the routes of transmission. Examples of good hygiene are given plus an audit tool to review facilities and practices. Specific safety advice for the baby room is given, as is information about childhood infectious diseases. It also considers the policies and permissions required and chronic disease management.

Key information

Calling the emergency services

Keep the following information by all telephones in your setting:

Dial 999 and request the service needed – fire, ambulance, police.

Provide the following information as asked:

+ telephone number of the setting;

+ postal address including the postcode;

+ the specific location within the setting, e.g. baby room;

+ your name;

+ the nature of the problem – if you need an ambulance give a short description of the child's symptoms along with their name and age;

+ the best entrance to enter the setting and say that someone will meet and direct the emergency crew to the location inside the building;

+ the name of the member of staff nominated to meet the emergency team.

How to wash hands effectively

Step one – wash hands with soap and clean, warm running water and rub your palms together.

Step two – wash each finger and thumb and interlock the fingers and wash the areas between them.

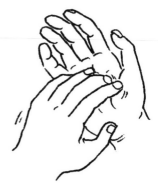

Step three – rub the tips of the fingernails on the palm of your hand.

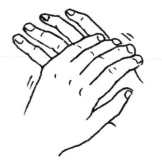

Step four – rub the back of your hands.

Step five – rinse your hands with clean, warm running water.

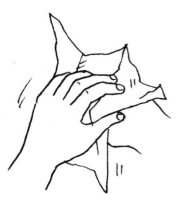

Step six – dry your hands with a clean paper towel.

How to do the meningitis 'tumbler' test

If a child is ill and gets a rash then you should:

+ check for spots over the child's whole body;

+ take a glass tumbler and press it firmly over the rash;

+ look through the glass tumbler – the rash will not fade if it is a septicaemic meningitis rash;

+ ensure that any child who is suspected of having meningitis is seen by a doctor immediately.

Part 1

Illness and Infection

CHAPTER 1

Preventing illness and infection

Introduction

Both staff and children may be incubating infections and while they may not feel ill they could be infectious to others. Infection is very common in children and is responsible for much of the illness in the under-five age group. Young children, especially those under the age of two years, need extra care and support as they are particularly vulnerable to their surrounding environment and infection. Hygienic practices, known as standard (universal) precautions, do help to reduce infections and illnesses spreading. Improving hygiene is one of the best ways to reduce the spread of disease.

This chapter provides information on how infections spread and the simple precautions that can be taken to reduce their transmission.

How infections spread

Breaking the chain of infection

Infections follow a sequence of events, which is often referred to as a chain of infection. All the links in the chain have to be intact for an infection to spread between people and cause disease. Following hygiene practices breaks some of these links and prevents disease spreading.

Microbes (aka germs)

Microbes are everywhere and a small number live in a symbiotic (mutually beneficial) relationship with us, inside and outside our bodies. This process begins when we are born and continues as we interact with other people and our environment throughout our lives. It is an important way in which our bodies provide natural protection against other types of microbes which can cause disease and make us ill.

How microbes spread

There are a number of different ways that microbes can spread between people. Some may spread through direct contact with body fluids of an infected person or from a mother to her unborn child in the uterus. Other ways include microbes spreading by indirect contact on the hands of people, by animals or on inanimate objects.

Routes of transmission

Microbes leave their host and are transferred to others through:

+ *The respiratory tract*, by inhalation. Small particles of dust or droplets can carry microbes into the respiratory tract through the nose and mouth. Examples of this include diseases such as tuberculosis, influenza and measles.

+ *Skin and mucous membranes*. Microbes can be introduced into the body by injection, bites, accidental injury or surgical incisions. Examples include Hepatitis B, malaria and tetanus.

+ *The placenta*. Microbes can be transferred from the mother's bloodstream to her baby across the placenta. This can cause congenital infections such as rubella and syphilis.

+ *The alimentary tract*. Microbes can be brought into the body on contaminated food and water. Examples include salmonella and polio.

Some microbes can use more than one route of transmission to cause infection. One example of this is hepatitis B, which is spread in three ways: as a sexually transmitted disease; or across the placenta to the unborn child; or through the skin and mucous membranes.

Mode of spread

Knowing the different routes of transmission for microbes helps to understand the way that infections are spread among individuals and the importance of following hygienic practices to prevent them.

The ways infections are spread between people include:

+ direct personal contact with contaminated body fluids especially on the hands of staff;

+ indirect contact with contaminated equipment such as nappies or potties;

+ carriers such as cockroaches, fleas, flies, mosquitoes and other pests;

+ coughing and sneezing;

+ spread from one part of a person's body to another such as the faecal-oral route when hands are not washed after going to the toilet.

The most important way that infections spread is by direct personal contact with hands contaminated by urine, faeces, blood, respiratory or other secretions. This is why washing hands is stressed as the most important thing to do to reduce and prevent illness and infection in yourself and others. How and when to wash your hands is described later in this chapter (see p. 16).

When is a child too sick for nursery?

Children who are already ill should not be taken to the early years setting due to the risk of passing on colds and other infections to others. If a child has any of the following signs or symptoms, they should stay at home:

+ fever, irritability, lethargy, persistent crying or difficulty breathing;

+ upper respiratory tract (the nose, throat and lungs) illness such as bronchitis, tonsillitis;

+ gastrointestinal tract (the stomach and bowel) illness with diarrhoea or vomiting (children should stay at home for 48 hours after their symptoms have stopped to make sure they are no longer infectious to others);

+ a rash that's linked to an infection (children are usually most infectious to others in the days just before the rash appears, once the rash appears they are usually considered to be less infectious to others);

+ bacterial conjunctivitis (see p. 94) until they have had 24 hours of antibiotics.

Immunity and immunisation

When children are enrolled in your setting you MUST ask their parents to complete a health record. This gives the child's full history of any allergies, medical conditions, childhood infections and immunisation record.

Because of the success of the national immunisation programme communicable diseases are very infrequent – which leads many parents to question whether vaccines are really still necessary. It is important to remember that these diseases haven't gone away and still cause outbreaks in other parts of the world. With the increase in holiday travel to distant places these diseases are only a plane ride away.

The infant immune system

The immune system in the newborn baby is very robust and designed to respond to the environmental challenges they meet in the first few hours and days of their life. While they have little natural immunity when born, babies have acquired some immunity from their mother. This immunity is then replaced through vaccination and interactions with others as they grow and mix in the world.

Concern is often expressed at the increase in the number of childhood vaccinations that are now given to infants. This implies that a baby's immune system is not able to handle vaccines safely or that multiple vaccines may weaken or overwhelm the immune system.

However, the infant immune system has an enormous capacity to respond safely and effectively to challenges from vaccines. While there may have been an increase in the number of combined vaccines given to babies they actually receive fewer substances in those vaccines than they did before. This is due to the improvements that have been made in vaccine technology.

Vaccines and how they work

Vaccines work by making the immune system produce antibodies to specific diseases without having to be ill with the disease. They work in two ways which are called either active or passive immunity.

Active immunity is when the vaccine triggers the immune system as though the body has been infected with a disease and teaches it how to produce antibodies, so if you come into contact with the disease itself, your immune system will immediately produce antibodies to fight against it.

Passive immunity works similarly to the immunity a newborn baby gets from its own mother when the antibodies are passed to the baby from the mother across the placenta. Rather than teaching the body to make the antibodies itself, with passive immunity specific antibodies are given so the body does not make them, but they last only for a short period of time, up to a year, when you need to be vaccinated again.

Vaccines are made in several ways using the same elements that are found in the natural virus or bacteria that causes the disease. There are a number of basic strategies used to make vaccines:

✛ *Attenuated vaccines* – this method weakens viruses so that when they are injected into the body they don't reproduce themselves very much and so don't cause the disease but they do make the body produce memory cells to protect against the infection in the future. Vaccines made using this method include MMR and are called live 'attenuated' vaccines.

+ *Inactivated vaccines* – this method completely kills viruses with a chemical so that when injected into the body they cannot reproduce themselves causing the disease. Polio, influenza and rabies vaccines are made using this method.

+ *Acellular vaccines* – this is where part of the virus or bacteria is used to produce the vaccine; an example is the Haemophilus influenzae B (Hib) vaccine. As with inactivated vaccines, 'booster' doses of the vaccine are needed every few years to ensure that immunity against the disease continues.

Primary vaccination schedule

By the age of four months children should have started their primary course of vaccines for diphtheria, tetanus, pertussis, polio, Hib and MenC followed by MMR at 12–15 months, and they will have completed the primary course by the age of five.

It is important to remember that immunisation protects us all from infectious diseases. The more people are immunised the less common are the diseases, but they have not gone away. If children are not immunised then the diseases can once again become common in society.

Vaccination schedule for England and Wales (2005/6)

Age	Vaccines
2, 3 and 4 months (primary course of immunisation with a total of 3 doses one month apart)	Diphtheria/Tetanus/Pertussis/Inactivated Polio/Hib (DTaP/IPV/Hib) one injection Meningococcal type C (MenC) one injection – 1st dose
12 to 15 months (can be given at any age over 12 months)	Measles/Mumps/Rubella (MMR) one injection
3 to 5 years (3 years after completion of the primary course)	Diphtheria/Tetanus/Pertussis/Inactivated Polio (DTaP/IPV or dTaP/IPV) one injection – booster dose Measles/Mumps/Rubella (MMR) one injection – 2nd dose
13 to 18 years	Tetanus/Diphtheria/Inactivated Polio (Td/IPV) one injection – booster dose

The importance of hygiene practices

There are a number of factors that influence the spread of infections and these include the prevalence of the disease in society and the number of susceptible children in the population. Alongside this is the knowledge and education of the staff working in the early years settings and that the environment should be safe, warm, light, welcoming and comply with health and safety legislation. This section highlights the main factors relating to children, staff and the environment.

Hygiene and children

Young children who attend early years settings are particularly susceptible to infectious diseases because of:

+ their young age and immature immune system;

+ the amount of close contact between children;

+ the lack of hygienic practices by children because of their young age and limited understanding;

+ sharing facilities and equipment;

+ their lack of previous encounters with infectious microbes;

+ their ability and wish to be agile and extremely mobile;

+ the decreasing maternally acquired antibodies;

+ the natural behaviour of children, their natural curiosity and intimacy with others;

+ bites and abrasions on the skin;

+ incomplete history of immunisation.

As well as these factors there are some children who are particularly vulnerable to infectious diseases because of their own medical conditions. These include those treated for leukaemia or other cancers, those treated with high doses of oral steroids and children who have conditions that affect their immune system reducing their ability to fight off infections.

It is important to remember that children with an infection will not only spread it among the other children in the early years setting but also to non-immune staff, their family and the wider community.

Oral hygiene

Poor dental health is a major problem in the UK due to the eating of food and drink which damages the enamel surface of the teeth. Children should be encouraged to:

+ take less sugary drinks and food;

+ brush their teeth after eating and before bedtime with a fluoride toothpaste;

+ have their teeth checked every six months by the dentist.

Hair care

Healthy hair is a sign of good diet. Frequent brushing helps to stimulate the circulation in the scalp. Hair routine involves regular cutting, washing and brushing:

+ how frequently hair is washed depends upon preference of the parents – at the most twice a week is sufficient to keep the hair clean along with washing it when it has become sticky or messy after any activity;

+ a gentle neutral pH shampoo should be used followed by rinsing well with clean water and drying with a towel;

+ some children dislike their hair being washed – wearing swimming goggles helps to keep the soap and water out of their eyes;

+ combs and brushes should be individual to each child and washed weekly.

See Chapter 8 (page 104) for information about managing head lice.

Hygiene and staff

Staff knowledge

Staff working with children should be suitably qualified or working towards a recognised qualification and supervised by an appropriately qualified person. The level of knowledge by staff and their awareness of infections can influence the spread of infection in early years settings. The Children Act 1989 suggests that half of the staff employed should have a child care qualification. They must also have at least 50 per cent of their staff with training specifically in caring for babies. It is important that the manager of the early years setting check qualifications and level of experience of their staff as not all qualifications cover the care of babies or include experience in caring for babies.

Staffing ratios

The Children Act also provides guidance on staffing ratios to allow for adequate supervision of children. For early years settings the minimum acceptable ratio is:

+ 1:3 for under-two-year-olds

+ 1:4 for two-year-olds

+ 1:8 for three- to seven-year-olds.

The number of staff employed must also be maintained at all times, wherever children are cared for, inside or outside, at meal times, rest times and staff breaks. Off-site visits need different ratios usually of:

+ 1:1 for children under one year of age

+ 1:2 for children between one and two years old

+ 1:3 for children between three and five years old.

Students on work placements must not be included in staff/child ratios and must be supervised by a qualified person. A high level of supervision of children during all their daily activities, especially feeding and toileting, should be allowed for.

Staff training

All staff when starting work should have induction training that includes health and safety and child protection policies and procedures within the first week of employment. Staff education is an essential part of preventing infectious diseases and should include information on:

+ common childhood diseases

+ modes of transmission

+ sources of contamination

+ infection control practices, especially hand hygiene

+ what to do if they themselves are ill.

Staff illness

Staff may also be susceptible to infectious diseases and an adult who is ill can be a risk by spreading the infection to children. Guidelines should be provided as to what to do if staff become ill and need to be restricted from doing certain care practices or excluded from work for a period of time. Employers are required under the Reporting of Injuries, Diseases and Dangerous Occurrences Regulations (1995) (RIDDOR) to report to the appropriate enforcing authority, which is either the local authority or the Health and Safety Executive when a member of staff is found to have a work-related disease.

Staff immunisation

Before starting work in the early years setting staff should make sure that they have been routinely immunised for:

+ polio

+ tuberculosis

+ diphtheria

+ tetanus

+ measles

+ mumps

+ rubella.

Female staff should also check that they have immunity to rubella, which can be achieved by having a simple blood test through their GP.

Personal hygiene for staff

One of the main sources of infection is ourselves, as microbes can be found on and in our bodies. Personal hygiene is not only important in staff but the National Standards require that the registered person of the early years setting informs staff of the importance of good hygiene and that children are encouraged to learn about personal hygiene through their daily routine. If staff do not practise high standards of personal hygiene themselves, they cannot lead by example or provide positive role models to the children they care for. Personal hygiene refers to washing hands and the body, being careful not to sneeze or cough over others and putting used tissues in the bin.

ACTIVITY:

Plan an activity on personal hygiene, which involves examples of good and bad hygiene. Could this then lead to a display by the children?

Managers of early years settings may at some time have to talk to a member of staff about their personal hygiene, which can be a difficult and sensitive issue. The most common problems that people have are:

+ body odour

+ halitosis (bad breath)

+ flatulence (excessive gas).

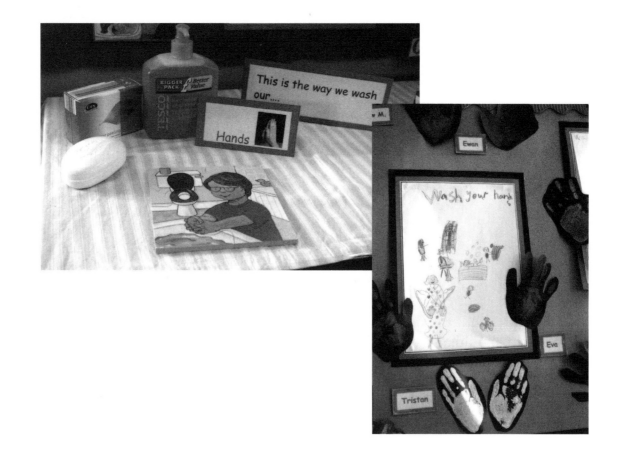

ACTIVITY:

Think how you might go about talking to a member of staff about their personal hygiene. Here are some approaches/phrases that may help:

+ Talk to the person on their own and ask if they have any problems with hygiene, dental health or dietary problems.

+ Some people have medical conditions that may result in excessive sweating that can be difficult to control and cause body odour.

+ Poor dental health can result in halitosis, such as bleeding gums or a decaying tooth, and they may have a fear of the dentist.

+ Poor diet or certain food intolerance can result in excessive flatulence.

+ If you have access to an occupational health service or school nurse they may as a neutral person be able to raise issues on behalf of the manager and not personalise the situation.

+ Often individuals with such problems are grateful for help and advice as long as it is given in a non-judgemental manner, as they may have tried a number of remedies without success and don't know what else to do; blaming someone for something they can't help doesn't resolve these issues.

+ If it is an issue of poor personal hygiene then having a uniform or hygiene policy allows you as a manager to discuss such concerns in a factual manner and relate it to the care of children.

Staff should maintain a high standard of personal hygiene by:

+ keeping the skin intact, reporting any skin conditions and getting treatment;

+ keeping the nails short so that they can wash their hands effectively;

+ covering the mouth and nose when coughing and sneezing and using disposable tissues, putting them in the bin immediately after use and then washing their hands;

+ washing their hands after going to the toilet;

+ not sharing toothbrushes with others;

+ not sharing towels, flannels or eye make-up;

+ only using towels and flannels that are clean;

+ covering any wounds with a waterproof dressing;

+ not sharing razors;

+ bathing regularly, washing their hair and daily changing clothes;

+ laundering towels, flannels and bedlinen every week.

Hygiene and the environment

The environment can influence how infections spread in early years settings and interventions are used to keep risks to a minimum. There are two key pieces of legislation that require early years settings to assess risk and to control hazards, including exposure to infectious microbes. These are the Health and Safety at Work etc. Act 1974 and the Control of Substances Hazardous to Health (COSHH) amendments Regulations 2004.

Studies have shown that not giving attention to the cleanliness of the environment results in widespread high levels of contamination particularly in the classroom, kitchen and toilet areas. Such high levels of contamination in the environment are then transferred onto the hands of children and staff and can be responsible for an increase in outbreaks of gastrointestinal infections. Consideration should be given not only to having strict cleaning protocols, but also to educating children about the importance of hand hygiene. Poor standards of cleaning and the lack of provision of soap, toilet paper and clean towels can increase the risk of diarrhoeal outbreaks.

Toilets that are kept locked to prevent children accessing them without supervision can result in children having accidents and contaminating the environment. Some children may also be reluctant to use a communal toilet and either have accidents or wait until they get home, resulting in medical problems of urinary tract infections and renal dysfunction.

Classroom carpets can be some of the most heavily contaminated areas of the environment and can be a cause for concern when children sit down on the carpet to listen to the reading of a story.

General routines

Good routines are important and include:

+ checking the premises at the start of the day before the children arrive to make sure they are clean and safe;

+ having a daily cleaning routine for all areas of the premises including the play areas, toilets, kitchens and nappy changing area;

+ having a cleaning protocol for toys, furnishings, dressing-up clothes, sand, water play area, ball pits and other equipment;

+ having suitable hand washing facilities available for staff and children;

+ providing separate rooms for babies and toddlers to rest, sleep and play;

+ placing cots at least 45 cm apart;

+ ensuring sufficient toilets (one per ten children) of child sizes with individual flushing mechanisms and toilet lids;

+ dedicating a nappy changing area with easily cleanable impervious surface;

+ providing written cleaning schedules to include
  - when something is cleaned
  - what equipment is used
  - whose responsibility it is to do it
  - what cleaning product should be used.

Do not routinely clean around children. Staff who are carrying out cleaning procedures should not be included in the adult:child ratio at the time.

Outbreaks of infection

Advice should always be sought from Environmental Health or Health Protection Nurses if you suspect you might have an outbreak of infection. The local hospital switchboard or your health centre should be able to provide a contact telephone number.

Facilities for babies

Within the early years setting there should be a separate base room for children under two years of age. Young babies need specific requirements and when planning such facilities consideration needs to be taken of their daily routine for feeding, playing, sleeping and hygiene.

The space required needs to accommodate:

+ nappy changing facilities

+ feed preparation area

+ play area

+ quiet area.

Space standards

Minimum space standards per child are:

+ under 2 years – 3.5 square metres

+ 2 years   – 2.5 square metres

+ 3–7 years   – 2.3 square metres.

Managing body fluids

Those who carry infection may be unaware of their condition and so the only sensible approach to preventing infections is to take sensible precautions and apply them universally to everyone and all situations.

Standard (universal) precautions should be followed by everyone and include:

+ hand hygiene;

+ wearing protective clothing of aprons and gloves when in contact with body fluids;

+ disposing of waste safely;

+ dealing with spillages;

+ safe handling of used linen;

+ cleaning of equipment and the environment.

The term body fluids is used to describe blood, urine, faeces and vomit.

The importance of hand hygiene

Hand washing is the single most effective way of reducing the spread of infections. This is achieved by removing or destroying microbes that have been picked up on the hands before they are spread to others. There are some diseases, especially those that cause diarrhoea type illnesses, which are easily spread on unwashed hands.

Research now shows that the viruses that cause colds while being spread between people in the air are more commonly spread between people on the hands after sneezing, blowing their nose or rubbing their eyes with unwashed hands. Thorough washing using soap and running water gets rid of most microbes from the hands and the earlier in life children are taught to wash their hands the better.

When to wash hands

Staff must wash their hands before:

+ starting work

+ preparing or serving food (including cooking activities)

+ feeding children

+ eating or drinking

+ caring for ill or injured children

+ putting on protective clothing (apron and gloves)

+ making up a bottle feed

+ taking bottles out of a steriliser

+ giving medication or first aid

+ leaving work.

They should wash their hands after:

+ going to the toilet
+ assisting children at the toilet
+ changing nappies
+ dealing with any body fluids (blood, faeces, urine, vomit, nasal secretions)
+ any cleaning procedure
+ caring for sick children
+ giving medication or first aid
+ handling soiled clothing or items
+ dealing with waste
+ removing disposable gloves and aprons
+ handling animals
+ handling high-risk raw food (chicken, raw meat)
+ planting or gardening activities
+ any activity in which the hands are physically soiled.

Children should wash their hands:

+ before eating, including snacks
+ before drinking
+ before cooking activities
+ after using the toilet
+ after playing outside
+ after playing with sand, water or dough
+ after touching animals
+ after planting or gardening activities.

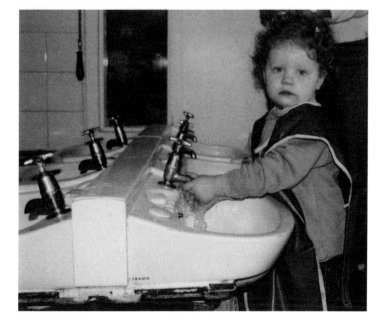

How to wash hands

When showing children how to wash their hands they should be taught that washing hands removes the germs that make them ill. A good hand washing technique is important as a lot of people miss parts of their hands such as the fingertips and thumbs.

To wash hands correctly:

✚ wet hands under warm running water (hot water must be regulated to deliver at a maximum 43°C to avoid scalding);

✚ apply soap;

✚ wash hands vigorously for 30 seconds paying attention to the fingertips, thumbs and in between the fingers;

✚ rinse well under running water;

✚ dry the hands thoroughly using disposable paper towels.

Step one – wash hands with soap and clean, warm running water and rub your palms together.

Step two – wash each finger and thumb and interlock the fingers and wash the areas between them.

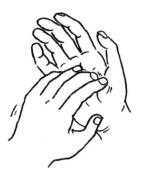

Step three – rub the tips of the fingernails on the palm of your hand.

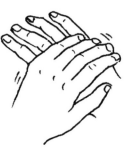

Step four – rub the back of your hands.

Step five – rinse your hands with clean, warm running water.

Step six – dry your hands with a clean paper towel.

Wearing of jewellery

The wearing of jewellery and the fashion for nail art should be discouraged, as it is a focus for microbes. Wearing gloves doesn't replace the need for hand washing and hands should always be washed before and after wearing gloves. Any cuts and abrasions on the skin should also be covered with waterproof dressings, protecting the injured person and others from the spread of infections.

Jewellery can also cause more immediate problems as young children may grab at necklaces, earrings or other piercings and this can cause bleeding.

Use of personal protective equipment

Normal everyday clothing or staff uniform does not provide sufficient protection when coming into contact with body fluids. Personal protective equipment should be made available to staff when there is a risk of contamination.

It is recommended that single-use disposable latex or vinyl gloves and disposable plastic aprons are worn for tasks where there is a risk of exposure to body fluids, such as:

✚ washing and changing babies;

✚ contact with contaminated clothing or toys;

✚ contact with contaminated equipment, changing mats, waste, potties.

Gloves

Disposable natural rubber latex (NRL) gloves should be powder-free and low in proteins to reduce the risk of allergy. It is important that staff are aware of the issues around latex allergy for both themselves and for others. Alternative synthetic gloves should be made available for any member of staff who has a latex allergy and should be worn by staff dealing with any child who has this condition.

Disposable aprons should be worn for changing nappies, emptying potties, cleaning toilets or during times when there may be splashing onto clothing. Disposable gloves and aprons must be discarded after each task and must never be used for more than one child. When removing used disposable gloves and aprons staff should take care to avoid contaminating themselves and their clothes. Hands must always be washed after removing protective clothing and before carrying out any further tasks. After disposable gloves and aprons have been used they should be placed into an appropriate waste bag.

Food handlers

Those staff who are food handlers should always wear clean protective clothing including headgear and hair nets if the hair is collar length or below. If other staff enter food preparation areas then they should wear protective clothing when in those areas.

Best practice checklist

+ Always wash hands before doing a clean task such as preparing food or drinks and after a dirty task such as going to the toilet.

+ Staff should maintain high standards of personal hygiene.

+ Suspected outbreaks of infection should be reported to the Environmental Health Department.

+ Personal protective equipment of gloves and aprons must be worn when staff are in contact with body fluids.

+ Staff should ensure their immunisations are current and up-to-date.

SELF-REVIEW ACTIVITY

One of the most useful practices that staff can encourage to reduce the spread of infection in children is to supervise them washing their hands. A classic study in 1981 showed that when a hand washing programme for staff and children was introduced the cases of diarrhoea were reduced by 50 per cent. A good hand washing technique taught young can protect a person against infection throughout their life.

Look at your current activities around hand washing for both staff and children; think how you can include practices throughout the day.

Activities include:

+ using finger paints to colour the hands before washing;

+ drawing round hands before and after washing the hands;

+ using a roll of wallpaper to get all the children's hands on one sheet for display;

+ adapting songs to wash hands to.

End-of-chapter summary

As microbes are found both in the environment and on people it is not possible for them to be eradicated. The role of immunisation in reducing infections within society has been effective over the years, resulting in what were considered as common childhood infections rarely being seen in the twenty-first century. However, if immunisations are no longer given then such infections can become common again.

Along with immunisation, the transmission of microbes can be reduced and cross-infection kept to a minimum by having high standards of personal hygiene that can be taught to young children. The most important way of preventing infections in early years settings is by frequent and effective hand washing by staff and children.

CHAPTER 2

Making and keeping a clean environment

Introduction

Everywhere in the environment there are microbes and the majority cause no harm to us. In the early years settings there is a need for a cleaning routine that controls microbes, odours and the spread of potentially infectious materials. Cleaning alone is usually sufficient for items that are in contact with healthy people.

This chapter will provide you with information on the different methods used to maintain a clean environment. Information on the risks to children associated with animals contaminating the environment, is discussed and a recommended protocol to follow for the general cleaning of the premises is suggested.

Environmental cleaning

Dictionaries define the word 'clean' as being 'free from dirt or stain'. We all wish to live in a clean environment and keeping our surroundings and environment free from dirt is a good starting point. The question of how to achieve it raises questions of what do we clean, how do we clean and how do we know that what we have cleaned is clean?

Dirt includes:

+ mud, earth, soil

+ faeces, vomit or other body fluids

+ dust

+ grease.

The ways of removing dirt include:

+ dusting

+ vacuuming

+ soap and water.

Routine disinfection of floors, furniture, fittings, worktops and other surfaces is unnecessary and may damage the surfaces. Cleaning alone is usually sufficient for items that are in contact with healthy people. You should have a cleaning routine that maintains the appearance of a clean setting and controls microbes, odours and the spread of potentially infectious material by the process of thoroughly cleaning and drying.

Cleaning and disinfection

Cleaning

The aim of cleaning is not to just redistribute but to remove soil and microbes from the environment. Some areas such as sink outlets, drains and toilet pans are heavily contaminated with microbes and cleaning is only a temporary influence, hence it needs to be repeated at regular intervals to maintain a certain standard of cleanliness. While these areas often cause concern and people spend a lot of money pouring down the drains disinfectants that are often ineffective, the risk of infection from these sites is extremely low.

Disinfection

Disinfection uses chemicals or heat to reduce the number of microbes in the environment to what is considered to be safe levels. It is usually used for equipment and surfaces that have been in contact with items or body fluids that may be infectious to others. How effective disinfectants are depends on effective cleaning before they are used so that they don't become inactivated by the body fluids or soil/dirt in the environment. It is important to choose the most appropriate chemical disinfectant and to use it correctly to decontaminate work surfaces, tables, toys, toilets, potties, teething aids and feeding bottles.

ACTIVITY:

Find out about the products that are used in your setting. What are they applied to?

Cleaning methods

Two methods of environmental cleaning are used: dry and wet. Dry methods use mechanical action to dislodge and remove dust. Wet cleaning methods are used on dirty hard surfaces and spillages. Wet cleaning is often preferred to dry cleaning as it doesn't raise dust, but it has its own risks of contaminating hands of staff and other surfaces if carried out incorrectly. A mixture of both cleaning methods often has to be employed because of the type of flooring and surfaces installed.

Dry methods

Dry methods include:

+ brooms
+ dust attractant mops
+ vacuum cleaners
+ dry dusting.

It is important to remember that once dust and dirt has been disturbed many allergens, such as dust mite faeces and feathers, can be raised by using dry cleaning methods.

Wet methods

Wet methods include:

+ scrubbing machines
+ mops and buckets
+ wet vacuum machines
+ disposable cleaning cloths for damp dusting.

There are risks associated with the use of wet methods for cleaning due to the use of water and chemicals. Equipment has to be cleaned and stored dry after use, as microbes like to grow in damp, moist conditions. Water used for cleaning has to be changed frequently otherwise, as with dry methods, microbes just get redistributed around the environment.

Disinfection methods

Heat disinfection

Heat disinfection methods are preferred because they are easier to control to achieve disinfection than using chemicals.

The reliability of these methods is increased when the temperature reached can be monitored regularly and articles cannot be accessed before the machine has completed its cycle.

Boiling: This is when items are heated to 100°C – that will kill the majority of microbes in less than a minute. Boiling water is used as a method to 'sterilise' baby feeding equipment but is not used regularly as microwave/steam sterilisers are the preferred method.

Particular care must be taken if boiling water is used in the early years setting. If possible carry out boiled sterilisation when the children are not present. If water must be boiled during opening times, ensure that children are not anywhere near the vessel, that the vessel is on a stable surface which is out of reach, and that any pouring/emptying of hot liquid is carried out within a sink so that it cannot spill. Never carry boiling water from one room to another.

Microwave/steam sterilising: There are a number of products on the market that 'sterilise' baby feeding equipment. Plug-in electric steam sterilisers take a varying amount of time, depending upon the make and model of machine, and work by using steam in a specially designed electrical unit. Items should be cleaned before being placed into the machine making sure that they don't touch each other. Water is added according to the instructions and the lid closed and secured before turning the machine on. The steriliser will turn itself off once the cycle has been completed. It should be allowed to cool before removing the lid and the contents. There is no need to rinse the items before they are used and if the lid is kept on they will remain clean for up to three hours.

Microwave sterilisers should be filled with water according to the manufacturer's instructions, the lid secured and placed in the microwave for the specified time and power level. When the cycle is completed it should be left to stand for a few minutes before removing it from the microwave and allowing it to cool before taking the lid off.

Cold sterilisation

The commonest method of sterilising baby feeding bottles is by the use of a 'Milton' cold sterilisation unit.

+ Make up a fresh solution every day following the manufacturer's instructions (the chemical is supplied either in tablet or liquid form).

+ The bottle and teat should be cleaned first using hot soapy water and then rinsed to remove all traces of milk using a clean bottle brush. Squirt water through the teat to remove any traces of milk.

+ Submerge the bottle and teat into the solution making sure no air gets trapped in the bottle or teat.

+ Leave the items in the solution for 30 minutes, making sure they remain submerged and in contact with the solution.

+ Remove the items and rinse in cold boiled water.

+ Store dry in a cupboard or drawer until needed.

Chemical disinfectants

Different chemical disinfectants are effective against different types of microbes. Not all disinfectants work on all microbes and there are a number of factors that affect how well a disinfectant will work.

Types of disinfectants

There are many different chemical disinfectants available for environmental cleaning and specific advice can be obtained from infection control specialists working for your health authority.

Recommended cleaning agents for the environment	
Disinfectant	**Environmental use**
Detergent and hot water	Routine cleaning of surfaces, tables, chairs etc.
Cream cleanser	Sinks, basins, tap handles
Hypochlorite (bleach) 1 in 100 solution (1000 parts per million)	For use if known infection risk, e.g. outbreak of diarrhoea, for disinfecting environmental surfaces (such as taps, toilets, potties and nappy changing mats) Also for spillages of blood and body fluids (but not directly onto urine)

Disinfectants should never be brought into the early years setting from home, nor should disinfectants be emptied out of their original containers, 'topped up' or mixed with other disinfectants. They should be stored under strict conditions, in a locked cupboard that only staff can access. Disinfectants must never be stored anywhere in the early years setting that children can access. Always read the labels carefully and measure amounts accurately.

Cleaning schedules

If there is an outbreak of infection in the early years setting then extra cleaning is recommended. All schedules should be reviewed on a regular basis.

Example of protocol for cleaning of premises

Item	Frequency	Method
General environmental surfaces	Daily	Manually clean surface areas at the start and end of the day and between use with detergent and hot water and dry thoroughly using disposable cloths/paper towels
Nappy changing mats and sleeping mats	After each use	Manually clean at the start and end of the day and between use with detergent and hot water and dry thoroughly using disposable cloths/paper towels
Hand wash basins, sinks, baths, bowls, toilets and potties	Daily and after each use for potties, baths and bowls	As above. Use cream cleanser for sinks, basins, baths as well as taps and toilet seats
Floors	Daily	Hot water and detergent (mop heads should be disposable or laundered after use) Vacuum-clean carpets to remove dirt and dust and steam clean regularly every 2–3 months Use disinfectants after contamination with blood spillages (not on carpets as it will remove colour)
Toys	Regularly	Soft toys – (daily and when soiled) on hot machine wash Hard toys – (weekly and after being put in the mouth by babies) with hot water and detergent, rinsed and dried thoroughly
Waste bins	Empty daily and also when full	Clean the inside with hot water and detergent when contaminated
High chairs, tables	Before and after use	Wipe with hot water and detergent and dry thoroughly
Walls, ceilings	Occasionally	With hot water and detergent

Furniture

Furniture is subject to wear and tear and spillages of tea, juice and other fluids, making it important to clean the tops of tables and high chairs before and after serving food; the material that furniture is made of must allow for frequent cleaning. Tables used for play or for preparing and serving food must not be used for changing nappies and children should never be allowed to climb or sit on tables; if it happens the tops of the tables should always be cleaned. Regular cleaning should also be undertaken on a routine basis as part of a general cleaning programme.

Carpets and flooring, soft furnishings

Carpets

The choice of floor covering depends upon the purpose of a room, with carpets being kept for office areas. Carpet cleaning should also be undertaken on a regular basis depending upon the amount of use it gets. Strong bleach is not recommended for use on spillages on carpets or furnishings as it can damage the colouring.

Flooring

Other floor surfaces should be of material that can be easily cleaned, especially in areas such as toilets and nappy changing areas where spillages occur.

Areas where toddlers and babies crawl or play may need extra attention and should be cleaned more frequently.

Walls, blinds and curtains

Cleaning of walls, blinds and window curtains is recommended when they are visibly soiled and an annual cleaning programme similar to spring cleaning at home is recommended to remove dust and surface grime.

Upholstered furniture and furnishings

Upholstered furniture and furnishings should be vacuumed regularly to keep dust and allergens to a minimum. A good practice is to replace upholstered furniture which has cloth covers with furniture that has covers that can be easily cleaned such as vinyl.

Nappy changing areas

When changing nappies it is an ideal opportunity for microbes to spread between babies and staff as they can contaminate the environment, changing mats and the hands and clothing of staff.

To prevent such levels of contamination it is important that staff:

+ wash their hands before and after changing nappies, even if gloves are worn;

+ wear disposable aprons and gloves and discard them after use;

+ clean the changing mat after use with a disposable cloth using hot water and detergent and dry thoroughly;

+ place used disposable nappies directly into an impervious bag, tied securely and then placed into a designated waste bin;

+ place towelling reusable nappies in a nappy bucket and flush the contents of the nappy down the toilet.

General issues to be considered include the following:

+ Changing mats should be checked regularly to make sure the covers are in good repair and thrown away when cracked or torn.

+ Tables and surfaces used for play, preparing and/or serving food should not be used to change nappies.

+ Barrier creams, if used, are for individual use and should not be shared between babies and toddlers.

+ Each child should have their own creams supplied by parents and appropriate to their personal needs.

+ Fingers should not be used to remove creams from containers use a clean disposable spatula each time.

+ Staff who prepare and serve food should not change nappies.

+ Nappy changing facilities should comply with environmental health standards.

+ Do not leave a child alone on a nappy changing table as they can roll then fall and injure themselves.

+ Scrupulous hand hygiene should always be performed to prevent infection spreading.

+ The nappy changing area should not be near where food is being prepared or served.

+ Make a checklist of all the equipment needed to change a baby's nappy and display it in the nappy changing area for staff to see and follow.

+ Keep notes of nappy changing routines for each baby.

+ Put a checklist in the nappy changing area for staff to sign to confirm that they have changed the appropriate baby's nappy and cleaned the area after use.

Discuss each child's requirements for nappy changing with their parents as nappy changing should depend on individual needs and not become a task where all babies are changed at the same time. Such methods increase the risk of spreading infection between babies, as staff are less likely to wash their hands or clean surfaces when there are a number of children needing changing.

Toilets, potties, nappies

Toilets should be kept clean and fresh by regular cleaning with detergent and hot water as often as necessary. Flushing the toilet removes the majority of microbes in the toilet bowl and regular cleaning prevents build-up. Just pouring disinfectants down the toilet does not remove microbes.

Children should always be supervised by staff when going to the toilet and encouraged to wash their hands afterwards. There is potentially a greater risk of spread of infection from toddlers with diarrhoea because they have no control over their bowels and need to rely on others to meet their hygiene needs.

How to clean these items hygienically

+ Toilet surfaces (especially flush handles) should be cleaned with a disposable cloth and hot water and detergent and dried thoroughly. When there is an outbreak of diarrhoea and/or vomiting then toilets and surfaces should be cleaned more frequently, paying particular attention to the seat and flush handles which should be cleaned after each use.

+ Changing mats should be cleaned with a disposable cloth and hot water and detergent and dried thoroughly immediately after use. If a baby has a loose stool or diarrhoea then an alcohol disinfectant wipe should also be used in between babies.

+ Potties, if used, should be emptied after use into the toilet bowl and cleaned using hot water and detergent and dried thoroughly before being stored away. They should never be stacked inside each other but be cleaned, dried and stored individually on a shelf.

Spillages

If a spillage occurs it is important that it is cleaned up immediately using hot water and detergent and disposable paper towels or cloths. Staff should wear protective clothing of gloves and apron and place all materials into a clinical waste bag. For spillages that involve urine, blood and other body fluids you should make sure that children are kept away from the area while they are dealt with.

Blood spillages

When cleaning up a blood spillage staff should:

+ put on gloves and apron;

+ cover the spill with paper towels and pour undiluted household bleach over them;

+ leave the towels for five minutes and then mop up the spillage with additional paper towels;

+ wash the area thoroughly with detergent and water;

+ put all the waste into a plastic bag, remove gloves and apron and put them into the plastic bag, then seal it and place it into a clinical waste bag;

+ wash hands.

It is important to remember that disinfectants are hazardous substances and should be used with care. Managers of nurseries have a legal responsibility under the Control of Substances Hazardous to Health (COSHH) regulations 2004 to carry out a risk assessment on their use and storage. Manufacturers must provide guidance on the product label and this must always be followed. Certain disinfectants such as hypochlorite (bleach) must be used in a well-ventilated area and should not be used directly on urine spills as they can cause a chemical reaction.

Spillages of vomit, urine, faeces

If there are any spillages of vomit, urine or faeces they should be cleaned up immediately. Before cleaning up a spillage staff should put on appropriate protective clothing (disposable gloves and aprons) and then gather together the cleaning material required, including impervious waste bag, to deal with the situation by:

+ covering the spillage with disposable paper towels to absorb the fluid;

+ mopping up the spillage by putting the paper towels into the waste bag;

+ clean the area with either mop or cleansing cloth, hot water and detergent

+ leaving the area to dry;

+ removing protective clothing into a waste bag and washing hands;

+ if the spillage is on the floor, putting a hazard warning sign out to warn others of the danger of slipping on a wet surface.

After any spillage, if there is any soiled clothing it should be placed into a plastic bag and then it can be cleaned on a standard machine wash cycle. Using a cold pre-wash cycle before the hot wash will help to remove any blood.

Laundry

Laundry equipment, if available, should be used in a separate room away from the kitchen area to reduce the risk of introducing faecal material into the kitchen. Industrial washing machines should be purchased rather than using a domestic washing machine as it is not possible to monitor the temperatures that the water and rinse cycles achieve.

If bedding, linen, towels and spare clothes are provided by your setting they should be laundered between use to prevent cross-contamination and infection and stored away from toilet and nappy changing areas.

Staff uniforms/articles of clothing with the nursery logo

If uniforms or special polo/T-shirts are worn and provided by the early years setting for staff, they should be given a sufficient number to wear a clean one for each shift. Staff should not travel to and from work in their uniforms and should change after arriving and before leaving work. They should wash them at the highest temperature permitted on the label and dry thoroughly.

Reusable nappies

Many early years settings send reusable nappies home for washing. If this is the case in your setting, the contents can be flushed down the toilet and the nappy placed in a plastic carrier bag, tied and stored safely while waiting for collection.

If reusable nappies are laundered on the premises, they should be soaked in a bucket of hot water and detergent for a short period of time before being washed in a washing machine using the pre-wash sluice cycle and then a hot wash.

The hygienic measures to be taken include the following:

+ Wear protective clothing (disposable gloves and aprons).

+ Remove solid material with a tissue and flush it down the toilet.

+ Use the pre-wash sluice cycle before using the appropriate hot wash cycle.

+ Wash used and soiled linen at 60°C or above.

+ Wash at 30–40°C with a bleach-based product.

+ Remove protective clothing and wash your hands.

+ Dry-clean linen in a tumble dryer and then iron.

Play equipment

Communal toys and the risks to children

Because children frequently put objects into their mouths, the risk of acquiring an infection from toys, especially those shared with other children, is increased. Toys often have porous surfaces and crevices where microbes can thrive.

Outbreaks of infection such as diarrhoea and hand, foot and mouth disease are easily spread in saliva and other bodily secretions.

Toys should be purchased that are easily cleaned and they should be washed between use by different children.

Keeping toys clean

Toys easily become contaminated with microbes from children, staff and the surrounding environment. Some viruses are particularly hardy such as rotavirus that causes the winter vomiting bug and other microbes in saliva that can survive on toys for 30 minutes. Contaminated toys include equipment such as play mats, plastic beakers and ball pools which all contribute to spreading infection. One outbreak of diarrhoea due to rotavirus in a day care centre found that 39 per cent of toy balls were contaminated with the virus.

Toys should be washed between use by different children and keeping toys hygienically clean is very important to prevent the spread of infection especially cases of diarrhoea and vomiting.

Water, sandpits, playdough and ball pools

Children should be taught to wash their hands before and after playing with any of the these items. During an outbreak of diarrhoea and vomiting these activities should be stopped as they increase the spread of the infection through contamination with the microbes.

After use:

✚ any water should be emptied from play equipment, and the equipment washed using hot water and detergent and dried thoroughly before storing clean and dry;

+ sandpits (both indoor and outdoor) should be covered to avoid contamination and the sand changed on a regular basis (once a month is considered appropriate);

+ playdough should be changed regularly and after contamination;

+ balls from the baby ball pool should be cleaned and dried every month and after any contamination from urine or faeces.

General management of toys

All toys should be stored away safely after use and not be accessible to babies and toddlers without supervision by a member of staff.

Make it regular practice to:

+ store toys in a clean container (with cover) or cupboard;

+ clean toys frequently and when soiled;

+ clean hard or plastic toys that are dirty or dusty by washing them thoroughly with hot water and detergent and storing them clean and dry;

+ wash soft toys when they are dirty in a washing machine after checking the cleaning instructions on the label first.

Hygienically clean contaminated hard toys by:

+ scrubbing the toy with hot soapy water and a brush;

+ rinsing the toy with clean warm water;

+ drying and wiping with an alcohol hard surface disinfectant wipe;

or by

+ scrubbing the toy with hot soapy water and a brush;

+ then soaking the toy in a mild bleach solution for 10 to 20 minutes;

+ rinsing it well in cool clean water;

+ drying well.

or by

+ putting them in the dishwasher or washing machine.

Outbreaks of diarrhoea and/or vomiting

Hard surface toys should be washed with hot water and detergent and then decontaminated with bleach solution (e.g. Milton solution) rinsed and dried thoroughly before storing away after use.

Hygienically clean contaminated soft toys by washing them on a hot wash cycle in a washing machine. Soft toys that are heavily contaminated really should be thrown away, no matter how fond the child is of it.

Animal visits

While pets are not routinely kept in early years settings it is important to understand the risk of infection associated with contact with animals. Infections can be passed from animals to children in a number of ways, such as via the fur, faeces and the environment. Activities such as touching and stroking animals need always to be followed by washing of hands by children.

Staff who are pregnant should be aware of the risks of infection when handling animals and should not handle litter trays as puppies and kittens with diarrhoea can pass on infection such as *Campylobacter*.

Animals should be exercised away from children and not be allowed into the kitchen or other food preparation areas. Any incidents of animal faeces must be cleaned up immediately and litter boxes must not be accessible to children. Particular care must be taken with reptiles and exotic pets as they can transmit infections such as salmonella, which can cause diarrhoea and vomiting.

Pests

The typical pests that can sometimes be found in buildings include:

+ cockroaches

+ flies and maggots

+ ants

+ spiders

+ mites

+ midges

+ mice

+ birds.

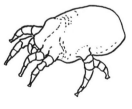

While there is no direct link of cause and effect between pests and disease, research does show that controlling the fly population leads to a reduction in diarrhoea among infants and young children.

Insects, birds and rodents can become agents for mechanically transferring microbes and spreading disease. Their habitats are marked by warmth, moisture and the availability of food. Insects forage on food scraps and routine household waste. Cockroaches and ants are often found in kitchens, storerooms and anywhere water or moisture is present, such as under sinks, drains and toilet areas.

Flies and wasps can be controlled by using insecticidal strips (not aerosol sprays in the kitchen) and traps can be used for mice and rats. Professional advice can be sought from the Environmental Health Department if you have a serious infestation of cockroaches, ants or other pests.

Disposal of rubbish

Risks to health

Risks to health from waste happen when:

+ waste is left to attract pests and flies and not immediately disposed of safely;

+ children come into contact with waste;

+ sharp objects such as glass cause injuries because they are not wrapped before being disposed of;

+ bins become a breeding ground for microbes because they are not kept clean and dry or frequently emptied;

+ waste spillages are not removed and the area cleaned thoroughly;

+ people do not wash their hands after handling waste or bins.

Duty of care

The duty of care is a law which requires every business in the UK to take 'all reasonable steps' to keep their waste safe. The objective of the duty of care is to protect people and the environment from illegally managed waste by creating an 'audit trail' of responsibility for the waste. The environment agencies and local authorities can follow the audit trail back to everyone who has been responsible for it. Prosecution happens if any party has failed to observe their responsibilities for the waste.

How to dispose of waste

✚ Clinical waste bins should be clearly labelled and marked as biohazard. These are managed by the waste contractor for your local council and should be used for waste from cleaning up spillages of body fluids or needles and syringes from diabetic children taking insulin.

✚ Use foot-operated bins with lids that fit.

✚ All non-contaminated waste should be placed in black bags within a foot-operated bin and disposed of as normal household waste.

✚ Aerosols, batteries or broken glass should be segregated from other types of waste and clearly marked before disposal by storing in individual boxes and contacting your local authority for advice on disposal methods in your area.

✚ All clinical waste should be removed from the premises by a contracted, registered waste company.

✚ Disposable nappies should be placed into the appropriate colour coded plastic bags for your area and disposed of as offensive waste by your waste contractor.

Best practice checklist

✚ Keep all disinfectants stored away from children in a locked cupboard.

✚ Have a cleaning routine and protocol.

✚ Use chemical disinfectants appropriately.

✚ Have a cleaning policy that states disinfectants to be used.

✚ Nappy changing areas should comply with Environmental Health standards.

✚ Have a policy for managing spillages, especially blood.

✚ Purchase toys that can be easily cleaned.

SELF-REVIEW ACTIVITY

Review your policy for toys purchased for your early years setting and how you would clean them so that they are hygienically safe for the children to use.

You may consider the following:

✦ Have you a policy and what does it recommend?

✦ Does it include anything about purchasing appropriate age-specific toys? And taking into account a child at a different/lower development level than their age?

✦ What does it advise about frequency of cleaning and how to clean?

✦ Do you have a washing machine to wash soft toys in?

✦ What recommendations can you make to improve safe practice?

End-of-chapter summary

The role of cleaning to prevent infection in the early years setting cannot be overemphasised. By putting in place simple policies and procedures that are followed by all staff, such as good hygiene practices, children can be protected from infection and diseases. It is important that premises are checked at the start of the day, are clean and safe before children arrive, and that hygiene procedures are included in staff induction and training programmes.

Safety in the baby room

Introduction

The most vulnerable children being cared for in early years settings are those under two years of age. The National Standards recognise the need for additional criteria for those caring for this age group. The implications of providing a safe environment for babies recognise that babies are totally dependent upon adults for all their needs. Not only should the physical environment be safe and secure it should also be adaptable to the different needs of each child and yet accommodate different areas for the different activities of nappy changing, feeding, sleeping and play.

This chapter provides information on the physical environment, safety issues of equipment, sleeping, nutrition and the common childhood conditions presented by young babies from cradle cap to diarrhoea. As with previous chapters there is a best practice checklist, self-review activity and summary at the end of the chapter.

The physical environment

The National Standards not only require that early years settings should be safe, secure and suitable but also apply additional criteria for those who wish to care for babies. These include making the room stimulating for young babies, having separate play areas for those babies that are mobile and those that are not, and how to integrate and get babies used to toddlers and older children.

Staff requirements

There are a number of requirements of those working with children under two years of age which include:

+ At least 50 per cent of staff have received specific training in working with the under-twos.

+ The person in charge of the baby room is experienced with this age group.

+ The children are cared for in groups of 12 or fewer.

The space

The minimum space that should be provided for each child in the early years settings are those quoted by the National Standards (DfES 2003) (see Chapter 1, p. 15).

The equipment

Cots

Any cot should comply with British Standards, with drop-down sides that have safety catches. The vertical bars spacing should be between 25 and 65 mm apart and the mattress fit snugly with less than a 40 mm gap. This ensures that babies cannot trap their head or limbs. The height should be deep enough (at least 500 mm) so that a baby can stand up in it without being able to climb out.

Once a child can stand up in a cot and climb out they should be moved into a bed, as it is no longer safe for a cot to be used.

Mattresses

Cot mattresses should also comply with British Standards specifying their construction and flame resistance. They should fit in the cot and provide a firm, flat sleeping surface. All mattresses should be kept cleaned and aired and turned regularly, preferably when changing the bedding, to maintain their shape. If they become soiled they should be cleaned following the manufacturer's recommendations.

Pillows, duvets, quilts and cot bumpers must not be used for babies under one year of age, as they are associated with an increased risk of SIDS (see p. 52).

Baby feeding equipment and teething aids

In many settings the parents/carers bring in bottles for their own babies and take the empties home when they collect their child. Staff should always ensure that the bottles are clearly labelled with the name of the child and the day's date.

If this is not the case in your setting read the following advice on correct methods of cleaning.

Bottles and teats and other infant feeding utensils, teething aids and dummies must be decontaminated between use either by boiling or by using a suitable disinfectant or sterilising product. Methods of disinfection include the use of a 'Milton' cold sterilisation unit using a solution that has to be made up fresh daily and changed if it is contaminated with traces of milk. A steam steriliser can also be used but you should add only the equipment recommended by the manufacturer and don't overload the steriliser as this can prevent sterilisation (see p. 25). Before any disinfectant or sterilising product is used all traces of milk must be removed from bottles and teats as otherwise the disinfectant becomes inactive.

Remember the following:

+ Wash bottles and teats thoroughly using detergent to remove milk traces and rinse in clean water before sterilising.

+ Make sure bottle brushes are thoroughly cleaned and then placed in the steriliser with the teats and bottles.

+ If using a cold sterilising unit, make sure all items are covered and immersed in the solutions for the length of time recommended by the manufacturer and that the solution is prepared according to the manufacturer's instructions.

+ Rinse off the sterilising solution using cooled boiled water, not tap water.

+ Wash hands before removing items from the steriliser.

+ Never add extra items into the sterilising unit once the recommended immersion process has been started.

+ Check bottles and teats and other equipment before they are used, if they are worn or damaged throw them away.

+ Always keep babies dummies and other equipment separate and labelled – never share dummies or bottles between babies.

Baby walkers and safety harnesses

Studies on the use of baby walkers have shown that they are responsible for more accidental injuries than any other type of furniture or equipment. Parents think that they help a baby to learn to walk but studies show increased evidence that this is incorrect and they may actually delay normal child development. The Royal Society for the Prevention of Accidents, Child Accident Prevention Trust and the Chartered Society of Physiotherapists all discourage their use.

High chairs are part of nursery furniture but it is important that any baby placed in these chairs is correctly restrained. The chair should have a wide base for stability and the Child Accident Prevention Trust recommend that a five-point harness should always be used with chairs, prams and pushchairs. If a three-point harness is used it should be tightly secured about the baby's waist.

Sleeping arrangements

These should be separate from other areas of the early years setting to allow for babies' and toddlers' individual sleeping patterns. Sleeping children should never be left alone and should always be observed and checked frequently to make sure that they are not too hot or cold. This is especially important for babies less than one year of age.

The sleeping area should have a suitable bed or cot for each child with clean bedding. The room should be kept at an ambient temperature (around 18°C) as babies especially should not be in a room where the temperature is too hot or cold. Try turning down the thermostat if the room is too hot or opening a window but not so that it causes a draught. You can also close the curtains or blinds to reduce the sunlight or move the cot away from the radiator.

Signs that a baby could be overheating include sweating, damp hair, heat rash, fast breathing, restlessness and fever. Feeling the tummy or neck of a baby can give you an indication if they are getting too hot or cold. Do not rely on touching their hands or feet as these would normally be colder than other parts of the body.

Remember:

+ Place babies on their back to sleep.

+ Never have soft bedding in the cot such as pillows, quilts or duvets.

+ Cover babies in layers of blankets which can then be added to or taken away depending on how hot they are.

+ A folded blanket counts as *two* layers.

+ Tuck the blanket in around the cot mattress and only let it reach as far as the baby's chest.

+ Make sure the baby's head is uncovered during sleep.

+ Place the baby in the 'feet to foot' position (see p. 54).

Nutrition and hydration

National Standards require that children must be given regular food and drinks sufficient for their needs. Adequate and nutritious food and drink is essential to a child's good health. Eating too little or too much or incorrectly balanced food can lead to illness. Eating healthily helps to make the immune system work effectively to fight off infection.

Breast milk or infant formula provides all the food and drink usually necessary for a young baby. Breast-feeding is thought to reduce the risk of gastroenteritis in babies. From one year old cow's milk can be given as a main drink and between meals. Other drinks that can be given include:

+ cooled boiled water between meals;

+ diluted fruit juice with ten parts water in a cup at meal times from six months old.

Remember to:

+ make toddlers aware that water is available at all times;

+ request information from parents and carers about children's dietary needs, preferences or food allergies;

+ plan menus in advance to take into account any dietary requirements;

+ wash fruit and vegetables before the children eat them;

+ keep a record of babies and toddlers food intake;

+ encourage parents not to give children sweets or sugary snacks or drinks to bring into the early years setting;

+ ensure that any food and snacks that are brought into the early years setting are stored at the correct temperature in the fridge until needed;

+ supervise toddlers at mealtimes;

+ ensure that babies are held while being bottle fed, preferably by their key-worker;

+ ensure that any milk left in the bottle after a feed is discarded and not re-used.

Safety issues

Babies are totally dependent on those who care for them so staff must be trained in first aid specific to the needs of babies. Staff should also be aware of serious medical conditions and communicable diseases common in babies and know the signs and symptoms of meningitis for babies and infants.

At each stage of a child's development hazards have to be reassessed for their level of risk. While babies can be contained and observed, once they start to crawl and walk different supervision is required and hazards should be eliminated or reduced to a minimum.

Once babies start to move they create dangers of their own by trying to climb out of cots, crawling around on the floor and touching and tasting things that they should not.

Babies and toddlers are unable to assess safety risks and lack co-ordination and balance. However, they do need to explore and this makes them vulnerable to accidents.

Particular safety issues include:

✚ equipment being appropriate to the age of the child;

✚ toys being appropriate for those under two years of age;

✚ use of safety harnesses for high and low chairs.

For more information on keeping children safe, refer to another book in the 'Health and Safety in Early Years Settings' series: *How to Keep Young Children Safe*.

Staff should never leave babies unsupervised whether they are sleeping or awake and should document and report any changes to the person in charge if they suspect medical advice may be needed. Contact details should be easily available for emergency help and to access parents quickly. Parents or carers collecting their children from the nursery must be informed of any symptoms.

Signs of illness include:

✚ vomiting

✚ temperature

✚ cough

✚ runny nose or eyes

or unusual behaviour of:

✚ crying

+ irritability

+ refusing food and drink

+ listlessness

+ drowsiness.

Exclusion periods

Every early years setting must have an exclusion policy that clearly states how babies and toddlers will be managed when they are ill.

This includes:

+ making the policy available to parents and carers;

+ informing other parents if there is any infection in the early years setting;

+ making parents aware that they need to tell the early years setting when their child has an infection or illness;

+ regularly updating the emergency contact numbers and children's medical details;

+ having contingency plans for when parents and carers cannot be contacted or cannot collect a sick child;

+ seeking advice from appropriate health services if unsure of current practice;

+ remembering that exclusion periods can also apply to staff in the early years setting.

First aid

Within the baby room there should be at least one member of staff who is trained in first aid for infants and young children. There should be a first-aid box available and with contents as recommended by the training course. It should be easily accessible but out of reach by children.

The minimum contents of the first-aid box should be as follows:

+ a leaflet giving general guidance on first aid;

+ twenty individual wrapped sterile adhesive dressings (assorted sizes);

+ two sterile eye pads;

+ four individually wrapped triangular bandages (preferably sterile);

+ six safety pins;

+ six medium-sized (12 cm x 12 cm) individually wrapped sterile unmedicated wound dressings;

+ two large (18 cm x 18 cm) sterile individually wrapped unmedicated wound dressings;

+ one pair of disposable gloves.

Tablets and medicines must not be kept in the first-aid box.

The nursery's first-aid procedures should identify the person responsible for maintaining the contents of the first-aid box, which should be checked frequently and restocked after use. A signed record of any accidents to children must be kept and Ofsted notified of any serious injuries or death. Further first-aid information is provided in Chapter 4 and in book two in this series, *How to Keep Young Children Safe*.

Common childhood complaints particularly affecting babies

Baby colic

This is common and distressing in newborn babies but usually stops by the age of three to four months. There are no medicines to stop colic but there are ways to help ease it in some cases. For no apparent reason babies with colic cry as if in pain and the usual methods of comforting does not seem to work. This can last for several hours until the baby settles and falls asleep. The term 'colic' is used as it is thought the baby has pain in its abdomen. However, the cause is unclear and nothing is found when examined by a doctor.

Ways to help colicky babies:

+ Create a relaxed atmosphere, staff should keep calm and not transfer feelings of anxiety etc.

+ Realise that overhandling might make things worse, if the baby is not hungry, wet or ill try to avoid holding the baby for long periods. A colicky baby cannot be comforted and it may be best to leave them in the cot for a short while to see if things settle.

+ Advise parents that there is a theory that lactose causes or aggravates colic in some babies. A doctor may be able to advise a trial lactose-free diet for a few days.

+ Parents might consider trying some of the following:
  - gripe water and infacol (over-the-counter medicines available from pharmacies)

- tapes of 'white noise' (like hoovering and the sound of a washing machine) which are commercially available
- car journeys – the white noise and gentle rocking may soothe.

However, there is little firm evidence for the effectiveness of these approaches.

Blockages

Children often stick things up their noses or in their ears. If you suspect they may have done this you should not try to remove the item, as you may push it in further. If the nose is blocked, you need to explain that they will have to breathe through their mouth until it is taken out. The child should be taken to the nearest Accident and Emergency department. (Toy safety is discussed in a partner book *How to Keep Young Children Safe*.)

Colds

Babies and toddlers may seem to always have a cold – it is considered normal for a child to have a cold eight or more times a year. This is because there are hundreds of cold viruses and children are meeting them all for the first time. Gradually as they get older they build up their immunity to them and get fewer colds.

Remember:

✚ Colds are caused by viruses not bacteria and so antibiotics don't help.

✚ Most colds get better in a week.

✚ Medicines for coughs and colds can cause side-effects in young children.

✚ Stuffiness can be made worse by nasal decongestants.

✚ Increase the amount of fluids that babies and toddlers drink when they have colds.

✚ Raising the head of the baby's mattress may help a snuffly baby breathe more easily.

✚ Increase the amount of hand washing by all staff as cold viruses are more easily passed between people on their unwashed hands than by sneezing and coughing.

✚ You can loosen dried nasal secretions or a stuffy nose with saline nose drops but check with your health visitor, GP or pharmacist and the parent.

✚ A teased cotton bud can be used to tickle the nose to cause sneezing to clear the nose in babies before feeding.

✚ Teach children to use tissues and to throw them into the bin once they have been used to blow or wipe their nose.

Coughs

Children may also cough when they have a cold because the mucus trickles down the back of the throat. If a child has a persistent bad cough their parents should take them to their GP as:

✚ if the cough is accompanied by a high temperature and/or breathlessness then the child may have a chest infection;

✚ a cough that persists for a long time and that is especially troubling at night may be a sign of asthma.

If the child is over the age of one year a warm drink of honey and lemon can ease a cough better than many commercially prepared cough medicines. While it may be distressing to hear children coughing, it is part of the body's defence mechanism and helps to clear phlegm off the chest. Older children can be taught to put their hands over their mouth when coughing so that their germs are not spread to others.

Cradle cap

The cause of this harmless dry scaly scalp condition is unknown. A white or yellow 'cap' is formed on the baby's head that can also affect the eyebrows. The cap is not itchy or irritating and the baby is well, and the condition eventually resolves on its own.

Croup

This is an inflammation of the larynx (voice box) and a child will have a hoarse, barking cough and noisy breathing. Sometimes croup can be life threatening so be aware of the danger signals. These include:

✚ breathing that has the air being drawn in between the ribs or below the ribs;

✚ restlessness and production of lots of saliva;

✚ irritability;

✚ blueness of the face and the lips.

If a child has any of these signs, the GP or an ambulance should be called immediately.

Diarrhoea

This is when the baby has frequent, loose, unformed stools often accompanied by vomiting. Both of these symptoms affect most young children at some time but it is important to check the amount of fluid lost. In babies the most common cause is a change to a baby's feed, or if breast-fed a change in the mother's diet. If a baby has diarrhoea it is important to maintain good hygiene particularly when handling soiled nappies and clothing, and wash your hands before and after handling the baby.

In mild cases of diarrhoea the World Health Organisation recommend:

+ feeding continues;

+ give extra drinks;

+ if the symptoms get worse call a doctor.

If a baby has severe symptoms of diarrhoea and/or vomiting it can lead to dehydration, where it is important to replace lost fluids quickly, and medical advice must be sought immediately.

Children with diarrhoea should in general:

+ have plenty of clear fluids;

+ eat if they want;

+ only have anti-diarrhoeal medicines when prescribed by a GP;

+ have separate towels from other children;

+ wash their hands after toileting and before eating.

Ear infections

Earache is common in babies and toddlers and often follows a cold where the middle ear becomes inflamed (otitis media). It is the commonest cause of severe pain in small children. Ear infections can result in a raised temperature and repeated infections may lead to 'glue ear' which is a build-up of fluid in the middle ear and stops the eardrum from vibrating properly, so affecting hearing.

Fever fits or convulsions (febrile)

Children under the age of three years commonly have 'fever fits' that are usually triggered by a high temperature. If a baby seems feverish, they should be cooled down immediately by:

+ giving plenty of cool clear fluids;

+ undressing them to their nappy;

+ covering with a sheet if necessary;

+ keeping the room cool.

For babies under six months old you should always contact the GP if they have a temperature of 39°C or above and if they have other signs of illness such as:

+ a fit;

+ they turn blue, or very pale, or seem floppy;

+ a rash anywhere on the body, especially one which is purple-red (this could be a sign of meningitis, see below and p. 97);

+ difficulty in breathing, breathing fast, grunting breathing;

+ drowsiness or being difficult to wake up;

+ a temperature, but with the hands and feet feeling cold and clammy.

If a child has a rash, always do the tumbler test as even a few single spots can mean that meningitis is present.

 Tumbler test: *press the side of a clear glass firmly against the rash; if it does not fade contact a doctor immediately.*

Meningitis

Most of us at some time will carry the bacteria that causes meningococcal meningitis and septicaemia (the blood poisoning form of the disease) at some time in our life, but won't get ill. We pass them between ourselves by regular, close or prolonged contact, which is how we build up our immunity. Babies and toddlers are at a greater risk of contracting meningitis or septicaemia than older children and adults. The early symptoms can be like any other childhood illness, but a baby will usually get ill more quickly and will become worse faster than older children and adults.

Always do the tumbler test if a child has a rash. Further information is provided in Chapter 6.

Nappy rash

Nappies should be changed frequently, especially after soiling, as it is important to keep the skin clean and dry. Most babies will get a nappy rash at some time or other which is usually mild and does not bother them and can quickly be cleared up with appropriate treatment.

Nappy rash is an inflammation of the skin usually due to a reaction of the skin to urine and faeces (soiling). As well as this a microbe called candida that causes thrush thrives on the inflamed skin. This can cause a more inflamed rash that may have darker red spots spreading around the nappy area. Most nappy rashes are not serious but occasionally some other skin conditions, e.g. eczema, psoriasis, can cause unusual nappy rashes.

To prevent nappy rash the following can help:

+ Fresh air – leave the nappy off as much as possible to get the air to the skin, the more fresh air the better. Try lying the baby on a towel or disposable absorbent sheet without a nappy for a while each day (don't forget to change the towel or sheet when it gets wet).

+ Nappies – change the nappy often and as soon as it becomes wet or soiled. The aim is to prevent long contact with the skin from urine and faeces. Washable nappies should be washed with a small amounts of detergent and rinsed thoroughly (but don't use fabric softeners).

+ Washing – water alone is best as soaps may irritate the skin.

+ Drying – make sure the bottom is properly dried before putting on a new nappy and dry by patting with a towel, don't rub.

+ Powders – these may irritate the skin so are best avoided. Talcum powder has also been linked to asthma in young children.

+ Barrier creams or ointments – these may help to protect the skin from moisture. Apply in liberal amounts at the first sign of redness to help prevent a mild rash getting worse. If you have parents' permission to apply it do so just before putting the nappy on.

+ Plastic pants – don't put tight-fitting pants over nappies as they keep moisture in and can make things worse

Treatments

If a nappy rash gets worse, advice to the parents from the health visitor or Doctor might also include the use of a treatment cream or ointment in addition to the above recommendations. If prescribed and permitted, any ointment or cream should be used sparingly after each nappy change and before a barrier cream is applied. It should not be used once the rash has gone.

The cream or ointment usually has an anti-thrush medicine combined with a mild steroid. The anti-thrush part treats the candida microbes and the steroid reduces the inflammation.

Sometimes nappy rash becomes infected with other microbes, which may need treatment with antibiotics. Always report the progress of any rash and let the early years setting manager know if it is becoming worse.

Poisoning

If you think a child has swallowed something poisonous, the emergency services should be contacted immediately. Salt and water should never be given to make the child sick. Observe the child closely for signs of loss of consciousness. The first-aider for the early years setting should be contacted in case the child needs resuscitation or becomes unconscious. If you know what poisonous substance the child swallowed, inform the emergency services.

Teething

Between four and nine months babies will begin teething and by the time they are one year they will have cut their first tooth. They may have flushed cheeks and dribble more, with the area of the gum looking red and inflamed.

While teething, babies may want to chew on things more, such as food, toys, fingers. They may also be more irritable and cry more and their sleep pattern can become disturbed. Babies should not be left with items to chew on because of the risk of choking, and any item given to a baby must be appropriate for the age of the child. It may be preferable to provide a teething ring or toy that has been sterilised and chilled in the fridge. Extra fluids can also be soothing.

Teething gels are available from chemists and advice can be obtained from the pharmacist. They should be sugar-free and the instructions must be followed regarding dosage and expiry dates. Parents' permission must be given.

Any paediatric analgesics that are used should only be done so on the guidance of the GP and will be appropriate to the age of the child.

Babies that dribble a lot may develop redness or a rash around the mouth, chin, neck and chest. The skin should be kept as dry as possible and wet clothing changed as needed, protect the skin by using a barrier cream.

Sudden Infant Death Syndrome (SIDS)

Cot death is uncommon and is rare after the age of five months; the term is used to describe a sudden and unexpected infant death that is unexplained. The medical term is 'sudden unexpected death in infancy' and a post-mortem is needed to identify the reason. Half of these traumatic cot deaths can be explained as accident, infection, congenital abnormality or metabolic disorder. For the rest there is no explanation and they are usually registered as 'sudden infant death syndrome' (SIDS).

Cot death can occur anywhere and at any time. It does usually occur during a period of sleep, but babies can die in their parent's arms or in a pram. It can affect any baby but certain babies are more at risk than others and these are the premature, the low birth-weight, and boys. It is not common in babies under a month old but increases in the second month with the risk getting less as they grow older. Approximately 90 per cent of cot deaths happen by the age of six months with very few occurring after one year.

Cot deaths can happen in any family, though it is more frequently seen in families who smoke or live in difficult circumstances. It is very rare for cot death to occur twice in the same family though an inherited disorder such as a metabolic defect may cause more than one infant to die unexpectedly.

Cot deaths can happen at any time of the year but do tend to happen in the winter months. The rates in the UK are similar to those in France, Norway and Sweden and have been decreasing along with those in industrialised countries in recent years following the introduction of Reduce the Risk campaigns.

Research has shown that the risk can be reduced and that prevention falls into three main categories:

✚ sleeping – learn the best way for your baby to sleep;

✚ smoking – create a smoke-free zone;

✚ symptoms of illness – if your baby is unwell seek medical advice.

Sleeping

✚ Lay the baby on their back to sleep, never on their front or side. SIDS is more common in babies who sleep on their front. There is no evidence that babies who lie on their back will choke. When babies reach the age of about five to six months and they are able to roll over, it is safe for them to sleep in whatever position they like, and it is at this age 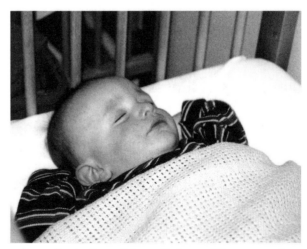 that the risk of cot death declines sharply. Babies like adults will toss and turn in their sleep.

✚ Do not use a pillow, a firm mattress that fits well into the cot is sufficient.

✚ Use layers of sheets and thin blankets rather than a duvet, loose covers or a 'baby nest'. These are more likely to cover the baby's face. Using thin layers allows them to be added or removed depending upon the room temperature.

+ Cover babies only up to their chest, leaving their head uncovered. Sheets and blankets should be tucked under the sides of the mattress to stop them riding up over the baby's face.

+ Maintain a safe temperature, babies need to be warm but not too warm. If the baby feels hot or is sweating, they are too warm.

+ Lay the baby 'feet to foot' with their feet touching the foot of the cot so they can't slip any further down under the blankets.

+ For parents it is best that a baby shares their parents' room until they are at least six months old, in a cot next to the bed. Cuddling and dozing with a baby should not happen if:

  – either parent smokes;

  – they are very tired or taking medication that makes them drowsy;

  – they have taken drugs or alcohol.

+ Falling asleep with a baby on the sofa has been shown to increase the risk of cot death.

+ Chapter 3, p. 42 discusses the importance of observing babies when they are asleep in the early years setting

Smoking

Cigarette smoking is a main risk factor for cot death so all early years settings are smoke-free zones. General advice is for no one to smoke in the same room as a baby and for women not to smoke while pregnant.

Symptoms of illness

Cot deaths usually are reported as happening 'out of the blue' when the baby is asleep with no symptoms to alert parents or carers that anything is wrong. Sometimes, however, an illness goes unrecognised and quickly gets worse. If a baby appears unwell you should always seek medical advice. The main symptoms to be aware for are:

+ vomiting, especially of bile (green) vomit;

+ taking less fluids (milk) or making less urine than usual;

+ high-pitched or unusual cry;

+ drowsiness, floppiness or being less responsive than usual;

+ wheezing, grunting, fast or difficulty in breathing;

+ high fever or sweating a lot;

+ their colour is pale or blue;

+ there is blood in the nappies;

+ rash.

Best practice checklist

+ All equipment, furniture and toys purchased should comply to current British Standards, fire and safety regulations.

+ Cots are never placed near windows or furniture that babies can climb on.

+ Baby feeding equipment and teething aids are kept separate and not shared between children.

+ Separate areas are designated for different activities of play, feeding, sleep and nappy changing.

+ There is one member of staff on duty at all times who is trained in first aid for babies.

SELF-REVIEW ACTIVITY

Consider the health and safety aspects of the baby room where you work. What policies do you have in place to make sure that the environment and the furniture and other items in it are safe for babies under the age of two years?

You may consider the following:

+ How do you maintain a constant room temperature?

+ When do you check equipment such as mattresses fitting the cot and their covers being intact?

+ Do you know the best way to lay a baby to sleep to reduce the risk of SIDS?

+ How frequently do you check babies when they are asleep?

+ How do you make sure that different babies' bottles, teats and teething aids don't get mixed up?

+ Do you know how to do the 'tumbler glass test' if a baby has a rash?

+ Can you quickly find the emergency contact number for the local GP?

+ Are cots in good condition?

End-of-chapter summary

Babies are totally dependent on adults for all their needs and those working in the early years setting need to understand the importance of maintaining a safe environment for them. This chapter has discussed not only some of the issues of the physical environment but also safety issues around equipment and sleeping. An introduction has been given to some of the common complaints encountered with young babies, including information about life threatening conditions such as Sudden Infant Death Syndrome and meningitis. Such information should help staff to plan activities and resources so that babies are safe in their care and have their needs met.

Managing illness

Introduction

Most early years settings will at some time need to consider how they will manage young children in their care who have a chronic medical condition. Legislation under the Health and Safety at Work etc. Act, Education Act, Medicines Act and the Children Act all have implications as to how such children should be cared for. Guidance on the management of children with special needs is given in the National Standards for Childcare for Children under 8. This chapter provides information on the more common medical conditions and how such conditions should be managed. There is also advice on food safety practices and the more common causes of food poisoning along with a best practice checklist for staff to assess their own practice. Finally a self-review activity asks about managing the care of a young child with asthma for staff to consider their own attitudes and policies on this issue.

Food safety practices

All staff responsible for preparing and handling food must be trained and be aware of and comply with food hygiene regulations.

Training should include:

+ food preparation
+ storing
+ cooking
+ serving food safely and hygienically.

It is extremely important that attention is paid to the hygienic preparation of food that is given to others, especially children and babies. Food preparation areas should be hygienically maintained and those working in them follow a high standard of personal hygiene. Everyone who prepares drinks, food or baby feeds is considered by Environmental Health to be a food handler and as such should have undergone a food-training course on the safe handling of food. Ideally, to make sure that there is no contamination of food and drink, those staff that are involved in toileting and nappy changing should not be involved in food preparation.

Mealtimes must be adequately supervised to make sure that babies and toddlers follow good hygienic practices.

Other considerations for food hygiene include:

+ establishing clear routines, rotas and staff responsibilities;

+ monitoring and reviewing food handling procedures;

+ providing a separate area for sterilising baby feeding equipment.

Staff must not handle food if they are suffering from:

+ skin infections;

+ sores;

+ diarrhoea and/or vomiting.

Food preparation areas

Early years settings should have purpose built food preparation areas, but it is important to remember that kitchen sinks should not be multi-purpose and should be used just for cleaning of kitchen equipment. There should be a separate sink specifically for hand washing only.

General kitchen hygiene rules

These include:

+ Wash your hands before preparing food.

+ Hygienically clean all work surfaces.

+ Clean all surfaces that hands touch, such as taps, handles, fridge door.

+ Use separate chopping boards for different foods.

+ Wipe high chairs, bibs and eating areas to remove food debris and hygienically clean them before serving food and drinks.

+ Use disposable cleaning cloths and throw away after use.

- Use disposable paper towels for hand drying and drying of crockery and cutlery.

- Use a waste bin with a lid to prevent access.

- Clean and disinfect the waste bin at least weekly, or more frequently if necessary, especially the handle and lid.

- Store food in airtight containers.

- Wash all cutlery and crockery in a dishwasher.

- Regularly clean the inside of microwaves.

- Regularly clean the fridge and freezer.

- Temperatures of fridges and freezers must be recorded daily.
  - fridge between 0 and 5°C
  - freezer below minus 18°C.

Managers are required to complete a food premises registration form from your local authority and an environmental health check as part of the registration process. If in doubt about whether you should be registered contact your local environmental health department.

Preparing food for babies and toddlers

Due to their developing immune systems, extra care needs to be taken when preparing food for babies and toddlers. This includes the need to:

- wash feeding bottles in hot detergent and water and sterilise using a sterilising solution or steam steriliser;

- always use cooled, boiled water when adding water to baby foods, milks and other drinks;

- cook food until it is piping hot and then cool rapidly until it reaches a comfortable temperature to eat;

- cook eggs until the white and yolk are solid or use pasteurised egg products – never give soft boiled eggs to young children.

Clean utensils

A dishwasher should be used to wash dishes, cutlery, cutting boards and kitchen knives and other equipment wherever possible after use. This should achieve temperatures of minimum 60°C. Heat drying or air drying in racks should be used or drying with disposable paper towelling that is discarded after use; linen drying cloths should not be used.

Hot water and detergent and disposable cloths should be used to clean worktops.

Utensils and receptacles can become contaminated after they have been cleaned when being stored. Knives for raw meat should be kept separate from those used for other foods. A colour-coded system is recommended for ease of identification to match utensils for tasks, e.g. red handles for raw meat. The same applies to cutting boards, to prevent the risk of cross-contamination.

First aid in kitchens

Managers must make sure that first-aid dressings are readily available to all food handlers according to the Food Hygiene (General) Regulations. Staff who have minor skin abrasions and are allowed to work, must have covered the area with a suitable dressing that is easily visible in most circumstances, such as a blue waterproof dressing.

Hydration in early years settings

Good health relies upon adequate hydration as the body is made up of 75 per cent water and dehydration is a major cause of ill health. A major study in 1999 found that we begin to feel thirsty at 1 per cent dehydration, our ability to work decreases at 2 per cent and lethargy, apathy and mental symptoms start to show at 4 per cent.

As a nation we don't drink enough water: adults have tea and coffee as common alternatives and children are given juices, colas and other fizzy drinks.

It is important to encourage children from a young age to drink, especially more water. Health practitioners are seeing an increasing number of children who are obese, enuretic (bed-wetting) and are at risk of becoming dehydrated with all the health risks that accompany it. The recommended amount of water for a five-year-old to drink is 1.5 litres every day.

+ Educate children about the benefits of drinking water by including it in the curriculum for healthy eating at Key Stage 1 (e.g. our cells need water for us to live, we lose water in sweat and urine).

+ Have a written water policy.

+ Actively encourage the drinking of water at snack and mealtimes.

+ Encourage children with colds to drink water, as colds can be dehydrating.

+ Make sure children drink water before and after exercising.

+ Give chilled water in summer.

+ On hot days encourage children to drink more water.

Food poisoning

Every year it is estimated that over five million people in the UK are ill from food poisoning.

Microbes causing food- and water-borne diseases are spread between people by eating and drinking contaminated food or water. The microbes are mainly bacteria and these germs can be found in:

+ raw food including meat, poultry, eggs, fish and seafood;

+ unwashed vegetables and fruit;

+ soil;

+ the guts of people and animals;

+ untreated water;

+ dust and insects.

Bacteria multiply fast and in the right conditions in eight hours one bacterium can become four million. They survive well between 5°C and 63°C but are killed at temperatures above 70°C. At low temperatures some bacteria will die but others just slow down and when the temperature starts to increase they begin to multiply again. That is why it is important to control the temperature of food to reduce the risk of food poisoning. At any point in the food chain microbes can contaminate food, from when an animal is killed or vegetables are pulled out of the soil until the food is put on our table to eat. Sometimes the microbes are transferred to our food on unwashed hands, kitchen utensils, chopping boards etc. and cause illness when we eat it; this is called cross-contamination.

Outbreaks of food poisoning

When outbreaks of food poisoning affect a group of people, such as in an early years setting, Environmental Health Officers (EHOs) employed by the local health authority will investigate to find out the cause. If there are a number of children or staff who have symptoms of diarrhoea and/or vomiting the manager of the early years setting should contact their environmental health department. An outbreak is classed as two or more people with the same symptoms. The EHO's role is to alert others to the dangers, provide advice and in certain cases prosecute people for breaching food safety laws.

The main reasons why food poisoning happen are:

+ not cooking food properly;

+ preparing food too far in advance;

+ storing food incorrectly;

+ cross-contamination in the kitchen;

+ people with infections preparing or handling food.

The following information is provided on the more common causes of food poisoning.

Common causes of food poisoning

Campylobacter

Campylobacter is the most commonly identified cause of food poisoning and is found in:

+ raw poultry and meat

+ unpasteurised milk (contamination can be from birds pecking the milk bottle tops on the doorstep)

+ untreated water.

Pets with diarrhoea can also be a source of infection.

Symptoms include:

+ fever

+ headache and a feeling of being unwell

+ abdominal pain and diarrhoea which might be bloody.

Symptoms take two to five days to appear but can take as long as ten days.

Salmonella

Salmonella is the second most commonly identified cause of food poisoning and is found in:

+ raw meat, poultry and eggs

+ raw unwashed vegetables

+ unpasteurised milk and dairy products

+ the gut and faeces of animals and humans.

Symptoms include:

+ fever

+ diarrhoea, vomiting and abdominal pain.

Symptoms take 12 to 48 hours to develop and can last for up to three weeks.

Infection can be very severe and in some cases fatal, especially in the very young and very old.

Escherichia coli

This is a widespread bacterium that is normally found in the guts of animals and humans. There are many different types capable of causing illness but the one that is causing particular problems, especially in children is Verocytotoxin producing E. coli 0157 and is found in:

+ raw and undercooked meats

+ unpasteurised milk and dairy products

+ raw vegetables

+ unpasteurised apple juice.

Symptoms include:

+ diarrhoea.

Symptoms take between two and five days to develop.

In children under the age of six years and in the elderly, infection can lead to bloody and severe diarrhoea, kidney failure and sometimes death.

Listeria

Listeria is present in the environment and one type, Listeria monocytogenes, causes illness in people and is found in:

+ soil

+ vegetation

+ raw milk

+ meat and poultry

+ cheeses (particularly soft mould-ripened varieties)

+ salad vegetables

+ the guts of animals and humans.

Symptoms include:

+ mild flu-like illness

+ meningitis and septicaemia.

It can take days or weeks for symptoms to develop and there are susceptible groups of people such as pregnant women, the very young and the very old. People in these groups are advised to avoid certain foods, such as soft cheeses and pates because of the risk of severe infection; especially pregnant women who can suffer miscarriage or premature birth of an infected child.

Chronic disease management

Early years settings should be aware of any child who has a medical condition. An individual healthcare plan should be developed with the parents and healthcare professionals so that the child's participation in activities is not unnecessarily restricted due to lack of staff knowledge. Sometimes the medical condition may become an emergency, needing immediate first-aid treatment. Having policies and procedures in place for the common medical conditions and including them in the induction and training of staff helps to provide a safe environment for children and staff.

Common medical conditions include:

+ allergies

+ anaphylaxis

+ asthma

+ diabetes

+ eczema

+ epilepsy.

Allergies

It is difficult to assess the number of children who may have an allergy. Allergies can be to foods such as peanuts, egg, milk, kiwi fruit, fish, soya and other substances such as latex and insect stings. However, it is likely that there will be at least one severely allergic child at your early years setting.

What is an allergy?

An allergy is an inappropriate response by the body's immune system to something which it thinks is a threat. The most severe type of reaction is anaphylaxis, which can be life threatening if not treated immediately with adrenaline.

What are the signs and symptoms?

Symtoms can vary, including:

+ itching or swelling in the mouth, or

+ an itchy rash all over the body.

Initially the symptoms may not be serious, but you should keep a close eye on the child in case the situation gets worse.

Serious symptoms include:

+ Swelling of the throat that makes breathing difficult and is a medical emergency.

Children who have asthma and an allergy are at an increased risk of having a severe allergic response. Staff should be aware of any child who has asthma with an allergy and it should be recorded in their healthcare plan.

If food is provided for children it is important to monitor the ingredients used, as even tiny traces of an allergen can be fatal for severely allergic children.

Practical guidance

+ Parents should provide safe food, including healthy snacks, which should be kept in a clearly marked container.

+ Do not let children have food from sources other than their parents or the nursery.

+ Have a separate table for children with peanut butter allergy.

+ Wipe tables and other surfaces after lunch.

+ Encourage children to wash their hands after eating.

+ Even a splash of milk or yoghurt may cause a skin reaction in children with milk allergies. Wipe up spillages immediately and thoroughly.

+ Children with egg allergies can have severe reactions so it is best to avoid using egg boxes or eggshells with them. Offer an alternative instead.

+ Do not use face paints on children with allergies as they may cause an unpleasant rash.

+ With children that have a nut allergy avoid making collages using nuts, seeds or pulses.

+ Staff training should include information on assessing signs and symptoms and how to give emergency medication.

Anaphylaxis

What is anaphylaxis?

Anaphylaxis is an extreme allergic reaction that can be life threatening and needs urgent medical treatment.

How does it affect a child's education?

Children who are aware from a very early age of what they can and cannot eat and drink often go through the whole of their school lives without incident.

What causes it?

The most common cause is food – in particular nuts, fish and dairy products. Wasp and bee stings can also cause allergic reaction.

Can it be treated?

In its most severe form the condition can be life threatening, but it can be treated with medication. This may include antihistamine, adrenaline inhaler or adrenaline injection, depending on the severity of the reaction.

Children are normally prescribed a device for injecting adrenaline, which looks like a fountain pen (EpiPen) and is pre-loaded with the correct dose of adrenaline given into the top of the thigh. It is not possible to give too large a dose using this device.

What are the signs and symptoms?

Each child is different and the signs and symptoms appear almost immediately after being exposed to an allergen and include some or all of the following:

+ swelling of the face, throat, tongue and lips
+ a metallic taste or itching in the mouth
+ difficulty in swallowing
+ flushed complexion
+ abdominal cramps and nausea
+ increased pulse rate
+ wheezing or difficulty in breathing

+ collapse or unconsciousness

+ widespread red, blotchy skin eruptions

+ puffiness around the eyes.

Practical guidance

+ If the child has an adrenaline pen, and staff are trained and permission given, administer the device.

+ If the child collapses or falls unconscious place them in the recovery position and remain with them until help arrives (be prepared to resuscitate if required).

+ Call an ambulance immediately if there is any doubt about the severity of the reaction or if the child doesn't respond to medication.

+ Keep adrenaline pens easily available to staff and always carry them on trips and visits.

Asthma

It is estimated that approximately one in eight children will have asthma, but it is no reason for them not to lead a full and active life.

What is asthma?

Asthma is a condition that affects the airways that carry the air to and from the lungs. Asthma varies in severity and while some children will have an occasional cough or wheeze others will have more severe symptoms. Sometimes the sleep of children can be affected due to asthma.

What are the signs and symptoms?

Symptoms include coughing, wheezing, tight chest and shortness of breath, though not every child gets all the symptoms. When a child with asthma has a cold or other viral infection or comes into contact with another trigger for asthma, because the airways are always inflamed they react badly to this.

What is a trigger for asthma?

Anything that irritates the airways can cause an asthma attack, every child's asthma is different, with different triggers, and most will have more than one.

It is important for children to know what triggers their asthma and that the early years setting is also aware of these triggers.

Common triggers include:

+ colds

+ viral infections

+ house dust mites

+ pollen

+ cigarette smoke

+ pets with fur or feathers

+ exercise

+ air pollution

+ laughter

+ stress.

What is an asthma attack?

When a child with asthma comes into contact with a trigger the lining of the airways starts to swell and secrete mucus, and the muscles start to tighten. This makes the airways very narrow, making it hard to breathe in and out normally. It is at this point that the signs and symptoms of asthma appear: cough, wheeze, tight chest and shortness of breath. It is at this point that the child will need to use their asthma medication.

What asthma medication is there?

Medication is usually given by reliever or preventer inhalers.

Reliever inhalers

These are usually blue and are the inhalers that children should keep with them at all times and should use whenever the asthma symptoms appear. Relievers work quickly and relax the muscles of the airways, making it easier to breathe.

Preventer inhalers

These are usually brown, white, orange, red or grey and white. They are either steroid or cromoglycate based. The steroid based preventers are low dose and extremely safe. Preventer inhalers are taken every day even when the asthma is well controlled, usually in the morning and evening.

Spacers

These make metered dose inhalers (spray inhalers) easier to use and more effective as they help more of the medication to be breathed straight into the lungs. Children under 12 years old find using the inhalers difficult without a spacer because of the need for co-ordination.

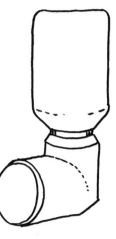

Practical guidance

If a child has an attack

+ Make sure they use their reliever inhaler straight away.

+ Stay calm and give reassurance.

+ Help them to breathe slowly and deeply.

+ Loosen tight clothing.

+ Sitting up or leaning forward slightly with their arms stretched wide (tripod position) helps most children to breathe easier.

After the attack

+ After a minor attack the child should be able to return to normal activities.

+ Inform the parents of the attack.

In emergency situations

Call a doctor or ambulance if:

+ the reliever has had no effect after five to ten minutes;

+ the child is distressed or unable to talk;

+ the child is getting exhausted;

+ there are any doubts at all about the child's condition.

Give reliever medication every few minutes until help arrives.

It is helpful if parents provide the early years setting with a spare inhaler for their child's use in case the inhaler is accidentally left at home or runs out.

Spare reliever inhalers must be clearly labelled with the child's name and stored safely. Medication provided for an individual child should never be used for other children. Help the child to pace their day if they have been losing sleep to asthma by offering rest periods or extra quiet times.

Diabetes

It is estimated that one in 700 children of school age in the UK has diabetes, often diagnosed around the age of five.

What is diabetes?

Diabetes is a condition where the level of glucose in the body is too high because it has lost the ability to produce the hormone insulin, which controls glucose.

What are the symptoms?

Without insulin the child's body is unable to use glucose, which makes the blood glucose level rise. Excess glucose leaks into the urine, making children pass urine frequently. They are also very thirsty. As the body can not use glucose it breaks down fats and this leads to weight loss. A child with undiagnosed diabetes will have symptoms of:

+ weight loss
+ unquenched thirst
+ frequent urination
+ tiredness.

What treatment is needed?

Diabetes cannot be cured but it can be treated, which includes injections of insulin and a balanced diet. The aim is to keep the blood glucose level within the normal range so that it isn't too high (hyperglycaemia) or too low (hypoglycaemia).

Insulin injections

Insulin cannot be taken by mouth so is given by injections, which are usually given before breakfast and before the evening meal. Some children may need to take an extra injection around lunchtime. The injections are given by either a syringe or a pen device. Recent research is studying the use of a form of insulin that can be inhaled through the lining of the nose, which hopefully will reduce the number of diabetics in the future who have to take injections.

Diet

The choice of food for a diabetic child is generally low in sugar and fat and high in fibre. This is so that the diet is a balance of different foods with particular attention to carbohydrates such as bread, rice, pasta, chapattis, yams, potatoes and cereals.

Children also need snacks between meals as they need to eat food at regular times during the day. If a meal or snack is missed or delayed it can cause the blood glucose level to drop, resulting in hypoglycaemia. It is important to allow children with diabetes to eat their food and snacks without making a fuss and explaining it to the other children.

What is a hypoglycaemic reaction?

A hypoglycaemic reaction is where the blood glucose level is low, and it is important to know what causes it, how to recognise the symptoms and the actions to be taken.

Common causes are:

+ missed or delayed meals or snacks

+ increased exercise above the normal level of activity

+ too much insulin for the amount of food given.

Each child's symptoms differ and the parents need to be asked how it affects their child. Signs and symptoms include:

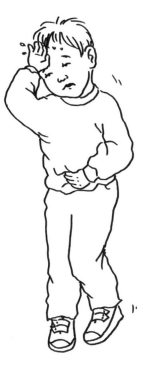

+ hunger

+ sweating

+ drowsiness

+ pallor

+ glazed eyes

+ shaking

+ mood changes or lack of concentration

+ rapidly deteriorating level of response.

How to manage a hypoglycaemic reaction

If a child is having a hypoglycaemic reaction you should give them fast-acting sugar immediately. Do not send children to get sugary food on their own, they should always be accompanied. Children with diabetes often have their own preferred fast-acting sugars and the parents should be asked for this information.

Examples of fast-acting sugars are:

+ Lucozade

+ sugary drinks, e.g. Coca-Cola

+ mini chocolate bar

+ fresh fruit juice

+ glucose tablets

+ honey or jam

+ 'hypostop', a glucose gel.

Should a child lose consciousness as a result of a hypoglycaemic reaction you should place them in the recovery position and call an ambulance informing them that the child has diabetes.

Recovering from a hypoglycaemic reaction usually takes about 10 to 15 minutes and the child may have a headache, feel nauseous or be tired. It is important to remember that hypoglycaemic reactions are a part of living with diabetes. However, if a child does have a reaction during school hours their parents should be informed.

What is a hyperglycaemic reaction?

A hyperglycaemic reaction is where a child's blood sugar level is very high (hyperglycaemia) and they become very thirsty and need to urinate frequently. They are also very tired and lose weight, which is often a sign that their diabetes is not well controlled. If their breath smells of pear drops or acetone it can be a sign of ketosis (when the body converts fats into energy) and they need to be seen urgently for medical treatment.

Eczema

In every early years setting it is very likely that there will be a number of children with varying degrees of eczema at any one time. Approximately one person in ten has eczema at some time in their life, usually when a child.

What is eczema?

Eczema is a condition where the skin can become dry, inflamed and occasionally weeping or infected.

Is it the same for everyone?

Eczema is a very individual condition that is different for every child and even the same child can have different skin conditions.

Where on the body can you get it?

It can be found anywhere though you usually see it on the backs of the knees, elbows, wrists, ankles and neck. In some cases eczema can be so severe that it covers the whole body and face.

What are the symptoms?

Eczema makes the skin hot and itchy and sometimes scaly. The skin can crack and become red and inflamed, making it prone to infection. Bacteria living on the surface of the skin can cause infections, resulting in weeping of fluid ('wet' eczema) with crusting or scabbing of sores. When the skin is itchy there is a great need to scratch with the greater the itch the greater the need to scratch. Scratching causes pain and bleeding but scratching doesn't relieve the itching. This itching sensation for some children is constant and it can be unreasonable to expect a small child not to scratch.

Is it contagious to others?

It is not contagious but because of how the skin can look children can be cruelly teased and be rejected by other children.

Does it ever improve?

As children get older it can improve, but it can reappear at any time, usually in adolescence or in times of stress.

What treatment is needed?

Because eczema is a dry skin condition it needs moisturising regularly. Dry skin itches and cracks, and smiling or moving the fingers can be painful. Applying emollients can relieve this.

+ When the skin is dry and itchy apply the emollient frequently.

+ Children with eczema can easily develop skin infections through contaminated pots of emollients, so always apply with clean hands and don't share pots of cream between children.

+ Apply a thin even layer of cream onto the skin, don't rub the skin as it can start off itching.

+ If using thick preparations use the dot method: apply small amounts where needed and use a spoon to smooth in gently from the top downwards.

What other treatments are available?

+ *Topical steroids* are applied to the skin to reduce inflammation in some children. Topical steroids aren't usually applied in the early years setting as most are applied once or twice a day, in the morning and evening.

+ *Antihistamines* may be given to children to help them sleep at night. This does make them drowsy in the mornings.

+ *Wet wrap bandages* are sometimes applied to the skin if children have severe eczema, impregnated with a soothing, messy paste. These bandages are put on at home but can need tidying up in the early years setting during the day.

Practical guidance

Scratching

+ Saying 'Don't scratch' does not work. Gently rubbing the skin may bring relief from itching without damaging the skin.

+ Emollient cream, a drink of water and a cool damp flannel might help.

+ Distraction and talk can sometimes calm an itchy child, along with reading a story or change of activity.

+ Carefully supervise the child when drying their hands to ensure they do it thoroughly.

Seating

+ Children with eczema should be seated away from sunny windows and radiators as itching can increase with overheating. Sitting on cotton material or folded towel minimises irritation from plastic seats.

Irritants

✚ Irritants include dusty conditions and animal fur, so affected children should be kept away from pets. Sitting or playing on carpet may also aggravate eczema.

Clothing

✚ The most comfortable clothing is cotton, especially next to the skin.

Meals

✚ Diet is very important; parents should be asked if there are any foods that make the eczema worse. There are a small number of children who may also have severe anaphylactic reactions to foods.

While children with eczema should be able to participate in the majority of activities with no difficulty, there may be times when extra care needs to be taken. Disposable gloves (vinyl, plastic or synthetic) can be worn by children when paint, glue, water, sand, playdough or other similar materials are used in sessions. It may also be useful to apply their emollient ointment before and after the session. Care should also be taken when using food in activities, as some food can be irritating to the skin, such as onions and oranges.

Epilepsy

Seizures (fits) in children under four years of age are usually caused by high body temperature. They are common but are not an indication that a child will have seizures for the rest of their life. However epilepsy affects over 300,000 people in the UK, with young people one of the common age groups that are affected by the condition.

What is epilepsy?

Epilepsy is a very individual condition that interrupts the electrical signals that are passed in the brain between the nerve cells. There are different types of seizures that include convulsions or strange or confused behaviour. Seizures are now no longer described as 'major' or 'minor' seizures but are called names that describe what is happening to the person.

The brain is divided into two halves called hemispheres, which are in turn divided into four lobes responsible for the different activities such as speech, smell, sight, emotions and movement.

Seizures may be partial (where consciousness is not necessarily lost, but may be affected) or generalised (where consciousness is lost).

Partial seizures

There are three types of partial seizures that affect part of the brain:

+ simple partial seizures (SPS)

+ complex partial seizures (CPS)

+ secondarily partial seizures (SPS).

Simple partial seizures (SPS)

With SPS the child is conscious and may know that they are having a seizure. It affects a small part of the brain and the child may present with either a twitch of a limb, an unusual smell, taste in the mouth (onions are often described) or the sensation of 'pins and needles'.

Complex partial seizures (CPS)

A larger part of the brain is involved and a child may present with confusion as consciousness is affected. Children may fiddle with their clothes or other objects, mumble or make chewing movements and wander about during this type of seizure. When talking to a child while they are having this type of seizure, be aware that while they will respond they won't fully understand or remember anything when it is over.

Secondarily partial seizures (SPS)

This term is used when simple or complex partial seizures spread to both hemispheres of the brain and the child becomes unconscious. The child may not be aware that their seizure began as a simple or complex partial seizure.

Generalised seizures

Generalised seizures occur without warning and affect both hemispheres of the brain, making the child unconscious. There are a number of different types of seizures including:

+ *Tonic clonic seizures* – this is the classic type of 'fit' where the muscles become rigid and the child falls to the ground and may be incontinent of urine or faeces and their breathing become laboured during the seizure. All children are different in the time they need to recover after the seizure.

+ *Absence seizures* – these last only a few seconds at a time and are short periods of staring, or blanking out. They are often so brief in nature that they may go unnoticed and children are accused of daydreaming or being unattentive.

Practical guidance

Classroom first aid guidance

+ Try to ease their fall.

+ Take a note of the time the seizure started and monitor how it progresses and how long it lasts.

+ Only move the child if there is a danger of sharp or hot objects or electrical appliances.

+ Cushion the head with a folded jacket, cardigan or jumper.

+ Don't restrain any movements.

+ Don't put anything between the teeth or in the mouth.

+ Turn the child onto their side into the recovery position to help their breathing when the convulsions (jerking movements) have stopped.

+ Loosen tight clothing around the neck.

+ As the child regains consciousness they may be confused as to what has happened so need reassurance that everything is OK.

+ After the seizure they may need somewhere to rest quietly and sleep for a while.

+ If they have been incontinent they will need to change their clothing.

+ Call an ambulance or doctor if this is the first time a child has had a seizure or if it lasts more than a few minutes.

+ Always inform the parents if their child has had a seizure during the school day, they do not normally need to be sent home afterwards but each child is different.

If possible a member of staff who is trained in first aid should stay with the child while another member of staff organises the other children and explains what is happening. Once the child has recovered they may wish to sit quietly in the room or return to the group and join in with the activities.

Emergency care

Medical help should ALWAYS be sought if:

+ the seizure shows no sign of stopping (the convulsions keep repeating without the child regaining consciousness) – this requires immediate medical support;

✦ a child who has no history of epilepsy has a seizure, even if it only lasts for a couple of minutes; the cause needs to be investigated, as it may be infection or a metabolic problem;

✦ they have injured themselves during the seizure;

✦ the seizure lasts two minutes longer than is normal for the child;

✦ the seizure lasts more than five minutes, especially if you do not know how long their seizure normally lasts.

Information from parents

If a child has epilepsy it is important to find out the following information from their parents to help with the management of a seizure during the school day.

✦ What are the types of seizures?

✦ How long do they last and what do they look like?

✦ What first aid is needed and how long do they need to rest afterwards?

✦ What particular conditions or events trigger a seizure?

✦ How often is medication needed and are there any side-effects to be aware of?

✦ Do they have a warning (aura) before they have their seizure?

✦ What activities do the parents limit?

✦ Have they any other medical conditions?

✦ What does the child understand of their condition and treatment?

Reye's syndrome

Reye's syndrome is a rare condition that affects the brain and liver in the under-fives and occasionally in older children up to the age of 19 years, though not adults. While it is not known what causes the syndrome the child can die within days or be left with a disability as there is no treatment available. Children seem to be affected when they are recovering from a viral infection such as flu or chickenpox and it appears to be linked to the taking of aspirin to control fever. The symptoms include severe vomiting, drowsiness or loss of consciousness following a viral infection. Since 2002 the recommendation has been not to give children under the age of 16 years aspirin or aspirin-containing products unless specifically advised by a medical doctor.

Best practice checklist

+ Medicines should be stored in their original containers, labelled with the child's name, dosage and time to be given, in a locked cupboard that is not accessible to children.

+ There should be written policies around administering and recording of medicines.

+ Staff should know how to identify emergency medical conditions and to contact the emergency services when necessary.

+ Have a quiet area for children who have a chronic medical condition that they can go to should they need to.

+ If there are a number of children who have to watch what they eat, have a whiteboard with their names and the foods to be avoided so that it can be quickly referred to by all staff at mealtimes.

+ Keeping a food history helps to identify foods that should be avoided for children with chronic medical conditions.

+ Obtain information from parents about what 'triggers' the individual child and their condition.

+ Asking parents to supply food in a plastic container clearly labelled with the child's name will help to ensure that they eat the food necessary to help control their condition.

+ Parents of children with asthma who use an inhaler should supply your setting with a spare reliever inhaler. This should be clearly marked with the child's name.

SELF-REVIEW ACTIVITY

David is a three-year-old child who attends your early years setting and has recently been diagnosed with asthma.

+ What is your asthma policy? Are you familiar with its contents?

+ What information have you asked for from David's parents about his asthma and his current treatment? Have you recorded this information anywhere and informed your colleagues?

+ How do you intend to tell the other children in David's class about his asthma and how they can help?

+ How are you going to educate staff about asthma, how it affects children and the treatment they need routinely and if they have an attack?

Points to consider

✚ You can either have a general policy that includes a number of medical conditions included as part of a health and safety policy, first-aid policy or health policy or their can be policies on individual conditions, depending upon the size of your early years setting.

✚ Use the individual health needs assessment tool (see p. 84) to draw up a health care plan for David. Records should be kept on David and his medication, all staff should know where this is kept and how to help David use it and what to do if he has an asthma attack. Children under the age of seven usually need help with their medication and their asthma inhaler should be clearly marked with their name and should be kept in an accessible place in the classroom or nursery.

✚ Further advice can be obtained from the school nurse and/or the asthma nurse specialist at the local NHS Trust.

✚ No child likes to be seen as different from others so it is important that other children in the class understand why David uses his medication and what they can do to help. Asthma UK provides ideas as to how it can be incorporated into the Primary National Curriculum in England and Wales in Key Stages 1 and 2.

End-of-chapter summary

Knowledge of chronic medical conditions by early years setting staff allows them to provide a safe and healthy environment for all the children in their care. Common themes can be identified in a number of conditions, such as the importance of making sure children eat appropriately to manage their illness. Through close observation staff can help parents in the identification of 'triggers' for their child's condition and so reduce the risk of a medical emergency and first-aid treatment. The normalising of such conditions into everyday life allows children to lead a more carefree existence and to fully participate in all early years setting activities safely.

CHAPTER 5

Record keeping and administering medicines

Introduction

Many young children are diagnosed with chronic diseases that require medicines to be given on a regular basis. These include asthma, epilepsy and eczema. Children who have such conditions need regular medicines to allow them to fully participate in life.

This chapter looks at the documentation that should be kept to record the practices followed for the administration of medicines to children. There are examples of forms that can be adapted, as well as a best practice checklist and a self-review activity.

Policies and permissions

Having policies on medication and children's medical needs helps not only to maintain their health and safety but for them to participate fully in all activities. It can also be a learning activity for staff. Policies need to be clear to staff and parents and should be included in the early years setting prospectus, or in other forms of information given to parents.

Before a child starts at the early years setting any long-term health needs should be discussed and a healthcare plan drawn up to inform staff of any care to be given. If children attend hospital appointments on a regular basis, special arrangements may be necessary around increasing staffing levels if an escort is required. Such arrangements could be included in the healthcare plan along with informing staff should a child want quiet time when they return and if one-to-one support is needed until they feel confident to mix with the other children.

If a child has to attend hospital appointments over a long period of time it could affect their individual development and this should be discussed with their parents.

Record keeping

Parents are responsible for supplying information about medicines that their child needs to take and for any changes to the prescription or support needed. Written details should be provided and include:

+ name of medication

+ dose

+ method of administration

+ time and frequency of administration

+ other treatment

+ any side-effects

+ any contraindications.

It can be helpful to give parents a form to record the details of medication in a standard format.

Parents' form for giving medication

Confirmation of the manager's agreement to give medication in the early years setting
(Example form for early years settings to complete and send to a parent if they agree to give medication to a child)

I agree that *[name of child]* will receive *[name of medicine and dose]* every day at *[time to be given]*.

[Name of child] will be given their medication by *[name of staff]* until *[either end date of course of medicine or until instructed by parents]*.

Date:

Signed: (named member of staff)

Review date:

(*Source*: adapted from *Managing Medicines in Schools and Early Years Settings*; Department for Education and Skills and Department of Health 2005)

Writing a health care plan

The reason for an individual health care plan is to identify the level of support needed for the child by the early years setting and its staff. A written healthcare plan states clearly for both staff and parents what help the staff can give. Health care plans should be reviewed on a regular basis to reflect the changes in a child's health and development. If there are no major changes then the plan should be reviewed annually.

Writing a health care plan should not be difficult or time consuming, though each plan will contain different details depending upon the needs of the individual child. A number of people can be involved in contributing to a health care plan and can include the:

✚ manager

✚ parent or guardian

✚ child (depending upon their age)

✚ staff who have agreed to give the medication or be trained in emergency procedures

✚ GP or other health care professionals (depending on the level of support the child needs).

A child's personal health record

Records offer protection to staff and proof that they have followed agreed procedures. A useful resource to refer to is the child's personal health record, known as the 'red book', which parents are provided with on the birth of their child. If kept up-to-date it includes information about:

✚ breast-feeding/bottle feeding and weaning;

✚ crying babies and behaviour;

✚ sleeping routines and reducing the chances of cot death;

✚ what to do if your child is ill;

✚ recognising meningitis and meningococcal septicaemia;

✚ immunisation;

✚ play and stimulation;

✚ dental care.

Individual health care plan

Individual health care plan for a child with medical needs
(Example form for individual health care plan)

Child's details:

1. Full name

2. Address

3. Date of birth

4. Medical needs

5. Any allergies

Contact details:

1. Name of parent/carer

2. Telephone number/mobile

3. Second contact name and number

Details of child's GP:

1. Name

2. Address

3. Telephone number

Medication:

1. Name(s) of medication

2. Expiry details

3. Where stored

Who is responsible in an emergency: (state if different on off-site activities)

Review date:

(*Source*: adapted from *Managing Medicines in Schools and Early Years Settings*; Department for Education and Skills and Department of Health 2005)

Administering medication

No child under 16 should be given medication without their parents' written consent. If in doubt about any of the procedures staff should check with either the parents or a health professional before taking further action.

Staff should complete and sign record cards each time they give medication to a child and having this witnessed by another member of staff is good practice to prevent mistakes occurring. It is also good practice that two members of staff check the medicine and dosage being given. Local authority controlled early years settings should follow their LEA's procedures on record keeping.

Example form for recording medication

Record of medication given in [name of early years setting]

(Example form for early years settings to record details of medication given to children)

Date	Child's name	Time given	Name of medication	Dosage given	Any reactions and type	Signature	Print name

(*Source*: adapted from *Managing Medicines in Schools and Early Years Settings*; Department for Education and Skills and Department of Health 2005)

Self-management

Children should be helped to take their own medication from an early age wherever possible. If children can take their medicine themselves, staff may only need to give supervision. The policy should say whether children could carry and administer their own medication, depending upon the safety of the other children.

Form for children to carry their own medication

Request for children to carry their own medication
(Example form for parents to complete if they wish their child to carry their own medication)

The parent must complete this form

Child's name:

Address:

Condition or illness:

Name of medicine:

Procedures to be taken in an emergency:

CONTACT INFORMATION

Name:

Daytime phone no:

Relationship to child:

I would like *[insert name]* to keep their medication on them for use as necessary.

Signed:

Date:

Relationship to child:

Review date:

(*Source*: adapted from *Managing Medicines in Schools and Early Years Settings*; Department for Education and Skills and Department of Health 2005)

Refusing medication

If children refuse to take their medication staff should not force them to do so. The parents should be contacted as a matter of urgency and if necessary the emergency services.

Non-prescription medication

Non-prescribed medicines should not be given to a child, as it is not possible to know whether they have already taken anything which might react with it.

A child under 16 years of age should never be given aspirin, unless prescribed by a doctor.

If a child suffers regularly from chronic pain their parents should authorise and supply appropriate painkillers for their child's use, with written instructions about when they should take them. A member of staff should supervise the child taking the medication and notify the parents, in writing, on the day painkillers are taken.

Safety management

Early years settings should make sure that medicines are stored safely and not given to anyone for whom they are not prescribed. The manager has a duty to ensure that the risks to the health of others are properly controlled under the Control of Substances Hazardous to Health (COSHH) amendments Regulations 2004 and the Reporting of Injuries Diseases and Dangerous Occurrences Regulations (RIDDOR) 1995 that require specific accidents, injuries and illnesses to be reported to the appropriate authority which is either the local authority or the Health and Safety Executive.

Storing medication

Large volumes of medication should not be kept on the premises and children should only bring the required dose of medication with them each day.

If medicine does need to be kept on the premises for some reason the manager should make sure that the container is labelled with:

+ name of the child

+ name and dose of the drug

+ frequency to be given

+ use by date (clearly marked).

If a child has two or more prescribed medicines then each should be in a separate container. Medicines should never be transferred out of their original containers. Responsibility for making sure that medicines are stored safely is that of the manager and children should know where their own medication is stored and who holds the key.

A few medicines, such as asthma inhalers, must be readily available to children and must not be locked away and preferably they should carry their own inhalers with them. However, it is essential that these medicines are not accessible to children other than for whom they have been prescribed. Other medicines should generally be kept in a secure place not accessible to children.

If medication that a child might need in an emergency is kept locked away, all staff should know where to obtain the keys to the medicine cabinet.

Some medicines need to be refrigerated and should never be kept in the same fridge as one that contains food or drink as they can become contaminated or may contaminate the food and drink. Local and community services pharmacists can advise on storing medicines safely.

Disposal of medicines

Medicines have to be disposed of safely. Parents should collect medicines at the end of each term and are responsible for disposal of medicines that are out of date. Advice about disposing of medicines can be obtained from community pharmacists and the local environment agency.

Emergency procedures

It is essential that all staff know how to call the emergency services (see p. viii) and who can carry out emergency procedures should they be needed. If a child is taken to hospital by ambulance then a member of staff should accompany and stay with them until their parents arrive.

Generally children should not be taken to hospital in a member of staff's own car. However, in an emergency it may be the best course of action. The member of staff must be accompanied by another adult and have public liability vehicle insurance.

Staff training

When writing a health care plan it is an ideal opportunity to assess whether staff need further information on medical conditions, giving a particular type of medication or in dealing with emergencies. Staff should not give medication without appropriate training from health professionals. If staff volunteer to help a child with medical needs, the manager should make arrangements with the Health Authority for appropriate training.

Example of staff training record

Staff training record – administration of medical treatment
(Example of form for recording medical training for staff)

Name:

Type of training:

Date of training:

Training provided by:

[name] has received the training detailed above and is competent to carry out any necessary treatment.

Trainer's signature:

Date:

Staff signature:

Date:

Review date:

(*Source*: adapted from *Managing Medicines in Schools and Early Years Settings*; Department for Education and Skills and Department of Health 2005)

Confidentiality

All medical information should be treated confidentially. Access to records and information should only be given to others on the agreement of the parents. If information is withheld from staff they should not generally be held responsible if they act incorrectly but otherwise in good faith in giving medical assistance.

Best practice checklist

+ Have a policy on administering medicines to children.
+ Have a policy on children who have regular hospital appointments.
+ Keep records of the type of medication a child has to take.
+ Provide written information to parents when agreeing to administer medication.

+ Complete an initial health care plan with parents about their child and update it as required.

+ Record when medication is given to a child and inform their parents when they collect the child as to what has been given and why.

+ Maintain a written record if a child has to carry their own medication such as an asthma inhaler.

+ If a child refuses to take their medication contact their parents to find out what effects this will have on the child. Record the incident.

+ Medicines should always be stored in a locked child-proof cabinet.

+ All staff should know where to find the key to the locked medical cabinet!

+ Medicines that are for one child should not be given to any other child.

+ All staff should know what emergency procedures need to be taken for children who take medicines.

+ All staff should know how to contact a child's parents in an emergency.

+ All staff working with children who have chronic diseases must be given training about the medicines they need and the individual nursery's policy.

SELF-REVIEW ACTIVITY

Imagine you have just started working at your early years setting. What training about medicines would be useful to your practice?

Ideas you may have considered:

+ the different types of medicines children take

+ how to store medicines safely

+ how to give medicines to children

+ what records need to be kept.

End-of-chapter summary

Providing medication in a safe manner to young children who have chronic diseases is important. Documentation such as healthcare plans and records of medication reinforces good practice of assessment and provides evidence of giving the correct medicine to the correct child.

All medicines should be stored according to current legislation and government guidance and not be accessible to young children. Staff who have agreed to give such medication should only do so after receiving appropriate training, which is updated (preferably on an annual basis).

Part 2

Specific Diseases

Signs and symptoms of common communicable diseases

Introduction

Children with an infection usually show general signs of illness before more specific signs occur such as rashes, spots etc. You should suspect that a child might be incubating an infection if they complain of the following: feeling unwell, shivering attacks or feeling cold, headache, vomiting or sore throat. In such situations the parents should be contacted and asked to collect their child. Advise them to consider consulting their GP if you feel it is necessary.

Exclusion policy

Every early years setting should have an exclusion policy to prevent and control infection based on the guidance provided by the Health Protection Agency. The purpose of such a policy is to prevent the spread of potentially infectious diseases between children and staff.

Some children are more vulnerable than others to infections due to having a medical condition. This includes those:

+ being treated for leukaemia or other forms of cancer;

+ taking high doses of oral steroids;

+ with any illness that affects their immune system.

An addendum to the National Standards was published in October 2005 stating that Ofsted should be notified of any food poisoning that affects two or more children on the premises, any child having meningitis and any outbreak in the early years setting of a notifiable disease (see Appendix 3).

The next sections provide information on the individual signs and symptoms of communicable diseases that staff working in early years settings may come across.

Common communicable diseases

Chickenpox

In children this is usually a mild viral infection that presents as a slight fever and itchy skin rash. The rash develops into blisters filled with fluid, which turn yellow and break and crust over. The rash can cover the whole body including the scalp, inside the mouth and eyes. Some children only have a few spots while others are covered.

Chickenpox is highly infectious and spreads quickly between people by direct contact with the spots, but it is also spread through the air by droplets from the respiratory system. The incubation period is between seven and 21 days, with children being most infectious two days before the rash appears and up to five days after the last blisters have appeared.

The same virus that causes chickenpox is also responsible for shingles (see p. 99).

It is important to remember:

+ Vulnerable children are susceptible to chickenpox and if they are exposed their parents should be informed so they can get specific medical advice if necessary.

+ Chickenpox can be a risk to any woman who is pregnant who has not had chickenpox themselves as the virus can be passed across the placenta to the unborn child – if this happens in early pregnancy (up to 20 weeks) or very late in pregnancy (three weeks before delivery) then they should see their GP or whoever is providing their antenatal care urgently.

+ Hands should always be washed after touching or treating the spots of an infected person.

Conjunctivitis

This is more commonly known as 'sticky eye'. The eye becomes watery and red and inflamed followed by a swelling and discharge of pus from the eye. It is spread by direct contact with the discharge and can also be spread by sharing items such as towels and tissues and is highly contagious. Treatment is by a course of antibiotic eye drops or ointment. The child should not attend the early years setting until the eye infection has cleared up. Should staff also acquire conjunctivitis they should seek treatment from their GP and remain off work until the infection has cleared.

It is important to remember:

+ Always wash your hands thoroughly after touching the infected eye.

+ The infected child should have their own towel and flannel.

+ Never share eye ointments, drops, tissues or towels.

Diarrhoea and vomiting

There are many causes of diarrhoea and vomiting in children, including a number of specific germs including viruses (rotavirus and norovirus), bacteria (salmonella, campylobacter, shigella and E. coli) and parasites (amoeba and giardia).

The most common cause of infection is through eating contaminated food or drinking contaminated water. It can also be spread between people by unwashed hands, especially in children.

Children and staff should stay away from the early years setting until their symptoms have ceased for 48 hours and they feel well.

It is important to remember:

+ Staff and children should pay attention to strict personal hygiene.

+ Always wash your hands after changing nappies or toileting children.

+ Always wash hands before meals and snacks.

+ Clean toilet seats and handles throughout the day and when soiled.

+ Stop activities such as water play, playdough, sand play and cooking if you have a serious outbreak of diarrhoea and vomiting in your setting.

Epiglottitis

The epiglottis is a piece of cartilage at the back of the throat that covers the larynx (voice box). When it becomes infected it swells and can obstruct the airways into the lungs. If this happens it is a medical emergency and the child should be seen and treated immediately. There are different bacteria that cause the infection, the most common being H. influenzae. Now that HiB vaccine is included in the primary immunisation schedule epiglottitis due to this bacterium is rare, though there are other bacteria and viruses that can cause it.

Epiglottitis usually affects children between the ages of one to six years, but it can be seen at any age. The symptoms of high temperature and sore throat appear quickly, making it hurt to swallow, and their breathing becomes difficult and noisy within hours. Children recover in a couple of days with appropriate treatment.

It is important to remember:

✚ This is a medical emergency and any child with symptoms of high temperature, difficulty in swallowing and breathing and sore throat should be seen by a doctor immediately.

✚ Vaccination has reduced the number of infections seen for the most common cause.

Fifth disease or slapped cheek syndrome (parvovirus)

This is a viral infection caused by the human parvovirus that affects the red blood cells. It affects anyone but is most often seen in schoolchildren and gets its name from the rash that appears on the cheeks making them look as though they have been 'slapped'. The infection is spread by exposure to secretions from the nose and throat from an infected person. The rash can extend from the face over the body, fading and then reappearing. Children are most infectious in the week before the rash appears, so excluding children is ineffective, as the infection has spread before the child becomes unwell.

It is important to remember:

✚ Always wash your hands after touching secretions.

✚ During outbreaks people with red blood cell disorders (such as sickle cell disease and thallaseamia) or women who are pregnant should consult their GP.

Hand, foot and mouth disease

This infection has nothing to do with the disease of foot and mouth in animals. It is a viral infection that affects children more than adults and outbreaks happen usually in hot summer weather. Symptoms include sore throat and fever followed by blisters and grey ulcers inside the mouth and on the palms and soles of the feet. In small children the rash can also affect the nappy area. It is caused by the Coxsackie virus and is spread by direct contact with the nose and throat secretions, faeces and fluid from the blisters of the infected person. It is usually a mild infection and children recover in a few days. There is no specific treatment or vaccine and no need to exclude children unless they are obviously unwell.

It is important to remember:

✚ Always wash your hands after touching secretions, faeces and blisters.

✚ Always wash soiled items promptly.

✚ Clean toilet seats and handles daily and when soiled.

Measles

This is a viral infection that is highly infectious and starts like a bad cold with a fever, runny nose, red eyes and cough. A red blotchy rash appears about three to seven days after the fever and spreads over the whole body. It is spread by direct contact with the secretions from the nose and throat. Immunisation is now available as part of the MMR vaccine.

It is important to remember:

✦ If a vulnerable child is exposed to measles the parents should be informed so they can get medical advice if necessary.

✦ Measles is more severe in infants and adults than children and complications include otitis media, pneumonia, croup, diarrhoea and encephalitis.

Meningitis

This is an infection of the linings of the brain by either a virus (usually a mild infection) or by bacteria, which can be a very serious infection. Most cases of bacterial meningitis in the UK are caused by the meningococcal bacteria. The child can become ill very quickly and not everyone has the same symptoms. The rash is very specific; and if a glass is pressed firmly against the skin and the rash can still be seen under pressure, this is indicative of meningococcal infection.

Meningitis is spread by direct close contact with the secretions of the nose and throat of an infected person. Those who have been in close contact with an infected person (household and kissing contacts) are treated with antibiotics as advised by the Consultant in Communicable Diseases. There is usually no need to treat contacts of children at early years settings. Exclusion is until the child is fully recovered and their GP says they are fit to return.

It is important to remember:

✦ Any child who is suspected of having meningitis must be seen by a doctor immediately.

✦ All cases must be reported to the Consultant in Communicable Diseases straight away.

✦ Siblings and other contacts of children diagnosed with meningitis do not need to be excluded.

Meningitis can progress quickly and be life threatening. It needs immediate medical treatment and symptoms include:

✦ fever (hands and feet may feel cold);

✚ refusing feeds, vomiting or diarrhoea;

✚ high-pitched moaning cry or whimpering;

✚ dislike of being handled, fretfulness;

✚ neck retraction with arching of back;

✚ blank and staring expression, bulging fontanelle (soft spot on the baby's head);

✚ being difficult to wake, lethargic;

✚ pale blotchy complexion;

✚ rash that does not fade when you roll a glass tumbler over it (the tumbler test); this can be as few as one or two spots.

Urgent treatment is needed with antibiotics and hospital admission for a child with bacterial meningitis. Those who have been in close contact with someone diagnosed with meningococcal meningitis may require prophylaxis antibiotics to prevent them getting the infection.

Research in January 2006 by the Meningitis Foundation identified key early symptoms which, if identified, could save lives.

Red flag symptoms:

✚ cold hands and feet;

✚ pain in limbs;

✚ abnormal colour, e.g. pale or mottled skins.

 Tumbler test: press the side of a clear glass firmly against the rash, if it does not fade contact a doctor immediately.

It is a good idea for early years settings to provide information leaflets for parents about meningitis, these can be obtained from the Meningitis Research Foundation (www.meningitis.org). Visits or talks to staff about meningitis can be arranged by contacting your Communicable Disease Nurse or Health Protection Nurse through the local Health Protection Agency.

Mumps

This is a viral infection that presents with fever and swelling and tenderness of the salivary glands in front of the earlobes. It is most infectious 48 hours before the symptoms start and the incubation period is approximately 18 days. It is spread by direct contact with the saliva and discharges from the nose and throat of children with the infection. Immunisation is now available as part of the MMR.

Rubella (German measles)

This is usually a mild viral infection that has a blotchy rash and slight fever. It is spread by direct contact with droplets from the respiratory tract of those with the infection. The child is infectious for one week before the rash appears until one week after. They should be excluded while they are ill until at least five days after the rash has appeared.

It is important to be remember:

✚ Rubella can affect the unborn child of women who are not immune to it and who are exposed to the infection during their early pregnancy. Female staff should have their immunity to the infection checked and any pregnant woman who comes into contact with rubella should see their GP. Notify parents of a rubella outbreak in the setting in case any of them are pregnant.

Shingles (herpes zoster)

This is seen rarely in children, as it is a recurrence of the chickenpox virus usually seen in adults. The rash follows the route of a nerve on the chest, abdomen or less often on the side of the head and face. It is very painful and it is infectious until the blisters have dried and crusted over.

It is important to remember:

✚ The rash can spread chickenpox to anyone who has not already had the infection.

CHAPTER 7

Other communicable diseases

Introduction

The diseases included in this chapter are serious to the individual child but may not be commonly seen by staff working in the early years settings. However, HIV, AIDS and hepatitis are transmitted through contact with blood and with body fluids that are contaminated with blood. As such it is important that staff are aware of the precautions to be taken when managing accidents safely.

AIDS (Acquired Immune Deficiency Syndrome)

This is caused by the Human Immunodeficiency Virus (HIV), which attacks the immune system and gradually destroys it, making the child susceptible to a wide range of infections.

Young children with AIDS or HIV infection may have acquired it in a number of different ways, such as being born to a mother with HIV infection or by receiving blood transfusions with products that were contaminated with the virus.

While no vaccine has been developed since HIV and AIDS were discovered over 20 years ago, the treatment provided means that those infected with the virus can live a normal life.

It is important to remember:

+ A child with AIDS/HIV is vulnerable *from* others who have an infection and they are not a major source of infection *to* others.

+ If the child has an accident that results in an injury that bleeds, staff should follow the routine precautions for managing all blood spills.

+ Their condition is lifelong and their schooling and other activities should be as normal as possible.

Diphtheria

This is a bacterial infection that affects the tonsils, throat and nose. It starts as a sore throat followed by a grey/white membrane that develops in the throat. The bacteria produce toxins (poisons), which cause death, or children die because the air passages are obstructed. Most cases come into the UK from abroad; it is a dangerous disease that has to be reported immediately to the Consultant in Communicable Diseases as part of the notifiable diseases legislation.

It is important to remember:

✚ Diphtheria can be prevented by immunisation.

Hepatitis (jaundice)

Hepatitis is caused by a number of viruses that affect the liver causing jaundice, a yellowing of the skin. The viruses are referred to by letters and are transmitted either by blood or by hands contaminated by faeces (faecal-oral route). The two most common infections seen in the UK are hepatitis A and B.

Hepatitis A

Hepatitis A is a virus spread by the faecal-oral route and symptoms include fever, loss of appetite, tiredness and abdominal pain. In adults these are followed by jaundice but many children never become jaundiced. Spread is by poor hygiene, especially lack of hand washing after going to the toilet. Outbreaks occur in nurseries and schools and children should be excluded for one week after they become jaundiced. It should be reported to the Consultant in Communicable Diseases as part of the notifiable diseases legislation.

It is important to remember:

✚ Practise strict personal hygiene.

✚ Wash hands after going to the toilet and before serving food and snacks.

✚ Clean toilets, including seats and handles daily and when soiled.

✚ Do not share towels or flannels.

✚ During an outbreak stop water play, playdough, sand play and cooking activities.

✚ There is an effective vaccine against hepatitis A.

Hepatitis B

Hepatitis B is rare in children and is a virus spread through blood and body fluids. The symptoms are similar to hepatitis A and a small number of people carry the virus in their body but don't become ill. The blood of people who are known as carriers is infectious to others and this is why blood spills should be treated promptly. It should be reported to the Consultant in Communicable Diseases as part of the notifiable diseases legislation.

It is important to remember:

+ Cover cuts and broken skin with a waterproof plaster.

+ Wear disposable gloves when dealing with blood and body fluids.

+ A vaccine is available for families and sexual partners of people with hepatitis B.

Poliomyelitis

This disease was once common in the UK but has almost been eradicated through immunisation. It is an acute illness that damages the nervous system causing weakness, paralysis or death. Spread is by close contact with an infected person, the virus is excreted in the faeces and if there is poor sanitation then this is also a means to spread the infection.

All cases have to be reported to the Consultant in Communicable Diseases as part of the notifiable diseases legislation.

It is important to remember:

+ Wash hands after going to the toilet.

+ If babies have received the live oral polio vaccine, extra care should be taken in washing hands after changing nappies as the vaccine is excreted in the faeces for up to five days.

Tuberculosis

This is a bacterial infection that usually affects the lungs (pulmonary TB) but can cause infection in other parts of the body. The symptoms are often vague and include weight loss, fever, especially at night, and a cough. The cough is the way that infection is spread to others. However, it is not easily transmitted to others and only a few cases are infectious. Treatment is effective and people are considered not to be infectious to others after two weeks of treatment. There is a vaccine called BCG, which gives a high degree of protection.

The length of time a child will be excluded depends upon the medical specialist and all cases have to be reported to the Consultant in Communicable Diseases as part of the notifiable diseases legislation.

Whooping cough (pertussis)

This is a bacterial infection that starts with an irritating cough and catarrh, which gets gradually worse, and the cough has a characteristic 'whoop' occurring in paroxysms. The child gets exhausted with the coughing and can damage the lungs. It is most infectious before the whooping begins and treatment by antibiotics reduces the period of time that it is infectious to others. Immunisation prevents the child getting the infection. A child with whooping cough should be excluded until seven days after treatment has started or 21 days after the paroxysmal cough.

CHAPTER 8

Contagious conditions of the skin and hair

Introduction

The conditions included in this chapter are often considered to be minor and of no consequence. However, they are frequently found in the community and persist, with children often becoming reinfected.

Athlete's foot

This is a common fungal infection that makes the skin between the toes itch. The skin becomes inflamed, cracks and may bleed. The infection lasts up to ten days if treated but can last for months or years if left untreated. There is simple effective treatment in the form of powders and ointments and advice can be obtained from the local pharmacist.

Prevention is by attention to personal hygiene of the feet by washing and drying them thoroughly, especially between the toes, followed by applying dusting foot powder to absorb moisture from the feet.

Head lice (nits)

These are tiny wingless insects that live on different parts of the body; those that are found in the hair are called head lice or commonly referred to as 'nits', which are the eggs of the head lice. The nits are tiny cream dots attached to the hair near the scalp and are very hard to dislodge. Tiny black specks can be seen on the pillow, which are the faeces of the lice. Head lice are spread by direct head-to-head contact with adults or children, they cannot jump, swim or fly. There is no need to exclude children but all contacts should be treated with the appropriate lotion and advice can be obtained from the school nurse or local pharmacist.

It is important to remember:

+ Treatment is only needed if live lice are seen in the hair.

- The best way to control head lice is for parents and carers to check the hair of children every week. Over a pale piece of paper and using a detection comb when the hair is damp, divide the hair into small sections and, starting with the teeth of the comb touching the scalp at the top of the head, draw the comb slowly down towards the end of the hair. If there are head lice in the hair they will be caught between the teeth of the comb or fall onto the paper.

- If a child is infected, their family will also need to be treated, and include grandparents and other relatives with whom they have prolonged contact.

Impetigo

This is a bacterial skin infection that becomes red, swollen, weeping and crusted and mainly affects the face but can occur anywhere on the body. Treatment is with antibiotics and children should be excluded until the lesions have dried up, if they cannot be covered with a dressing.

It is important to remember:

- People with impetigo must not handle food.

- Hands should be washed thoroughly after contact with lesions or contaminated items.

- There should be no sharing of items such as clothing, bedding, towels etc.

Ringworm

This is not caused by a worm but is a skin infection caused by a type of fungi and appears as a flat, spreading ring-shaped area. Spread is by direct skin-to-skin contact with an infected person or animal or by contact with contaminated items such as combs, hairbrushes, towels etc.

It is important to remember:

- Always wash hands after contact.

- Do not share towels, clothing, pillows etc.

- Showers, baths and other communal areas should be cleaned regularly.

Scabies

This is an infestation by a tiny mite that is very common. The mite burrows into the webbed skin between the fingers and causes irritation that leads to scratching. Spread is by close contact, such as holding hands; the mites cannot live outside of the skin and cannot jump between people or live in the environment. If a child is diagnosed as having scabies then it is important that all those in close contact, such as their family, are also treated. Once a child has had a course of treatment they can return usually the next day.

It is important to remember:

+ Itching can last for one to two weeks after treatment and does not mean the treatment has not worked.

+ Outbreaks of infection can occur where staff may also need to be treated as well as the child and family.

+ Avoid games that involve holding hands if there is scabies in your setting.

Verruca

This is the term given to a wart on the sole of the foot that is painless and disappears over time. If it becomes painful or spreads it may need treatment. There is no need to exclude children but it should be covered if children go swimming, play in a paddling pool or take part in activities that are done in bare feet.

Worms

There are a number of different types of worms that live in the human gut. The two most common types in the UK are threadworms and roundworms. Eggs are transferred from the parasites on the hands to the mouth where they are swallowed and hatch in the gut. Here the female worms lay their eggs in the faeces or around the anal area. Poor hand washing and scratching of the anus allow eggs to be caught under the nails, and the eggs are then transferred onto objects or food or into the mouth.

Threadworms are very common but may not cause symptoms. However they may cause disturbed sleep due to itching around the anus, irritability, scratching and often soreness. Diagnosis may be made by seeing the worms, which are like threads, around the anus, especially at night before bathing or going to the toilet, and also in the faeces.

Eggs remain infectious for about two weeks and treatment should be for all the family, but there is no reason for keeping a child away from the early years setting as long as good personal hygiene is followed and treatment is carried out.

It is important to remember:

+ Wash hands thoroughly after going to the toilet.

+ Keep nails short and clean.

Useful contact details

The Anaphylaxis Campaign
PO Box 275
Farnborough
GU14 6SX
Tel: 01252 542029
Email: info@anaphylaxis.org.uk
Web: www.anaphylaxis.org.uk

British Allergy Foundation
Deepdene House
30 Bellegrove Road
Welling
Kent
DA16 3PY
Tel: 020 8303 8525
Fax: 020 8303 8792
Email: allergybaf@compuserve.com
Web: www.allergyfoundation.com

British Diabetic Association
Macleod House
10 Parkway
London NW1 7AA
Tel: 020 7424 1000
Fax: 020 7424 1001
Email: info@diabetes.org.uk
Web: www.diabetes.org.uk

British Epilepsy Association
New Anstey House
Gate Way Drive
Yeadon
Leeds LS19 7XY
Tel: 0113 210 8800
Fax: 0113 391 0300
Email: epilepsy@epilepsy.org.uk
Web: beehive.thisisbristol.com

Cancerlink
17 Britannia Street
London WC1X 9JN
Tel: 020 7833 2451
or
9 Castle Terrace
Edinburgh EH1 2DP
Tel: 0131 288 5557

Contact a Family Contact Line
(information source for parents of
disabled children and all professionals
working with disabled children)
209–211 City Road
London EC1V 1JN
Tel: 020 7608 8700
Fax: 020 7608 8701
Web: www.cafamily.org.uk

Cystic Fibrosis Trust
11 London Road
Bromley
Kent
BR1 1BY
Tel: 020 8464 7211
Email: enquiries@cftrust.org.uk
Web: www.cftrust.org.uk

Early Support
Royal National Institute for Deaf
People
19–23 Featherstone Street
London EC1Y 8SL
Tel: 020 7296 8000
Text: 020 7296 8001
Fax: 020 7296 8199
Email: informationline@rnid.org.uk
Web: www.taylorsmith.ltd.uk

Hyperactivity Children's Support
Group
71 Whyke Lane
Chichester
West Sussex
PO19 2LD
Tel: 01243 539966
Email: hyperactive@hacsg.org.uk
Web: www.hacsg.org.uk

MENCAP (Royal Society for Mentally
Handicapped Children and Adults)
117–123 Golden Lane
London EC1Y 0RT
Tel: 020 7454 0454
Email: information@mencap.org.uk
Web: www.mencap.org.uk

National Asthma Campaign
Providence House
Providence Place
London N1 0NT
Tel: 020 7786 4949
Email: mediaoffice@asthma.org.uk
Web: www.asthma.org.uk

National Eczema Society
Hill House
Highgate Hill
London N19 5NA
Tel: 020 7281 3553
Fax: 020 7281 6395
Web: www.eczema.org

National Reyes Syndrome Foundation
of the UK
c/o Gordon Denney
15 Nicholas Gardens
Pyrford
Woking
GU22 8SD
Tel: 01932 346843
Fax: 01932 343920
Email: gordon@reyessyndrome.co.uk
Web: www.reyessydrome.co.uk

The National Society for Epilepsy
Chesham Lane
Chalfont St Peter
Bucks
SL9 0RJ
Tel: 01494 601300
Fax: 01494 871927
Web: www.epilepsynse.org.uk

Royal National Institute for the Blind
105 Judd Street
London WC1H 9NE
Tel: 0845 766 99 99 (for the price of a
local call, UK callers only)
Tel: 020 7388 1266
(switchboard/overseas callers)
Fax: 020 7388 2034

Scope
PO Box 833
Milton Keynes MK12 5NY
General switchboard: 020 7619 7100
CP Helpline: cphelpline@scope.org.uk
or call 0808 800 3333
Web: www.scope.org.uk

SENSE
11–13 Clifton Terrace
Finsbury Park
London N4 3SR
Tel: 020 7272 7774
Text: 020 7272 9648
Fax: 020 7272 6012
Email: info@sense.org.uk
Web: www.sense.org.uk/

The Sickle Cell Society
54 Station Road
London NW10 4UA
Tel: 020 8961 7795
Fax: 020 8961 8346
Email: info@sicklecellsociety.org
Web: www.sicklecellsociety.org

Audit tool

Infection control checklist for review of facilities and practices

Facilities/practices	Yes	No	Comments
Separate sinks for staff and children			
Liquid soap and paper towels available			
Hot and cold mixer taps with temperature control valves fitted			
Foot operated lidded bins available for all waste			
Adequate nappy changing facilities with sink, soap, paper towels and foot operated lidded bin for waste			
Protective clothing available			
Alternatives to NRL gloves are made available where there is a latex allergy issue			
Individual child named toiletry items (no sharing of personal items, medicines or clothing)			
All floors, surfaces are made of impervious material for cleaning			
Carpets are not fitted in toilet, nappy changing, laundry or food preparation and serving areas			
Reporting systems are in place for repair/maintenance for equipment			
All children have a written individual health care plan where appropriate			

Facilities/practices	Yes	No	Comments
48-hour exclusion rule is followed for children and staff suffering from diarrhoea and vomiting			
Use of disposable wipes for children at toileting and mealtimes when hand washing is not appropriate for wiping hands and mouths			
Written records are kept for administering medicines, sickness records, exclusion periods			
Staff training records are kept for first aid, infection control, health and safety			
Comprehensive policies are available to staff for: ✚ Cleaning ✚ Spillages ✚ Use of disinfectants ✚ Use of protective clothing ✚ Nappy hygiene ✚ Sickness and exclusions ✚ Management of outbreaks ✚ Food hygiene ✚ Farm/zoos outings ✚ Pets ✚ First aid ✚ Used linen and soiled clothing ✚ Waste ✚ Toys and play equipment ✚ Hand washing ✚ Staff health and training			

Diseases notifiable (to Local Authority Proper Officers) under the Public Health (Control of Disease) Act 1984 and the Public Health (Infectious Diseases) Regulations 1988

Acute encephalitis

Acute poliomyelitis

Anthrax

Cholera

Diphtheria

Dysentery

Food poisoning

Leptospirosis

Malaria

Measles

Meningitis
meningococcal
pneumococcal
haemophilus influenzae
viral
other specified
unspecified

Meningococcal septicaemia (without meningitis)

Mumps

Ophthalmia neonatorum

Paratyphoid fever

Plague

Rabies

Relapsing fever

Rubella

Scarlet fever

Smallpox

Tetanus

Tuberculosis

Typhoid fever

Typhus fever

Viral haemorrhagic fever

Viral hepatitis
Hepatitis A
Hepatitis B
Hepatitis C
other

Whooping cough

Yellow fever

Leprosy is also notifiable, but to the Director, CDSC

Bibliography

'All about asthma: school pack (2002)' [online] available at www.asthma.org.uk [accessed 01/11/05].

'Allergy in schools' [online] available at www.allergyinschools.org.uk [accessed 01/11/05].

Committee on Safety of Medicines (CSM) (2002) Consultation letter: MLX 290 'Aspirin and Reye's Syndrome: proposal to introduce a statutory warning following advice from the committee on safety of medicines'. London: Department of Health [available online at www.mhra.gov.uk/home/groups/comms-ic/documents/publication/con007618.doc accessed 01/11/05].

Department for Education and Employment (DfEE) (1996) 'Supporting pupils with medical needs in school' [online]. Circular number 14/96 [available at www.dfes.gov.uk/publications/guidanceandthelaw/14_96/summary.htm accessed 01/11/05].

Department for Education and Skills (DfES) (2003) *Full Day Care: National Standards for under 8s day care and childminding*. Nottingham: Surestart, DfES.

Department for Education and Skills (DfES) and Department of Health (2005) *Managing Medicines in Schools and Early Years Settings*. London: DfES Publications.

Department for Education and Skills (DfES) (2005) *Full Day Care: National Standards for Under 8s day care and childminding*. Nottingham: Surestart, DfES.

Department of Health (1990) *The Children Act 1989*. London: Department of Health.

Department of Health (1999) 'Guidance on infection control in schools and nurseries' (poster and leaflet). London: Department of Health.

'Diabetes in schools' [online] available at www.diabetes.org.uk/teenzone/school.htm [accessed 01/11/05].

'Epilepsy – a teacher's guide' [online] available at www.epilepsy.org.uk/info/teachers.html [accessed 01/11/05].

Health and Safety Executive (HSE) (1992) *Personal Protective Equipment at Work Regulations*. London: HMSO.

Health and Safety Executive (1995) *The Reporting of Injuries, Diseases and Dangerous Occurrences Regulations (RIDDOR)*. London: HMSO.

Health and Safety Executive (HSC) (1999) *Management of Health and Safety at Work Act Regulations 1999*. London: HMSO.

Health and Safety Executive (2004) *Control of Substances Hazardous to Health (COSHH) amendments Regulations 2004*. London: HSE Books.

Health Service Advisory Committee (HSAC) (1974) *Health and Safety at Work etc. Act*. London: HMSO.

Holmes, E. 'Hydration in schools' [online]. DfES [www.teachernet.gov.uk accessed 01/11/05].

'Information on epilepsy' [online] available at www.epilepsynse.org.uk [accessed 01/11/05].

Office for Standards in Education (Ofsted) (2001) *Childminding: Guidance to the National Standards*. Nottingham: DfES.

Office for Standards in Education (Ofsted) (2001) *Full Day Care: Guidance to the National Standards*. Nottingham: DfES.

Office for Standards in Education (Ofsted) (2003) *Day Care: Guidance to the National Standards. Revisions to certain criteria*. Nottingham: DfES.

Offit, P.A. *et al.* (2002) 'Addressing parents' concerns: do multiple vaccines overwhelm or weaken the infant immune system?' Children's Hospital of Philadelphia, USA [accessed 2/4/05 at www.sciencedaily.com/releases/2002/01/020109073542.htm].

Parker, L. (2006) *How to Keep Young Children Safe*. London: David Fulton Publishers.

Parker, L. (2006) *How to Do a Health and Safety Audit*. London: David Fulton Publishers.

Ross, S. (2003) 'Nurseries and schools'. In: Lawrence, J. and May, D. *Infection Control in the Community*. Edinburgh: Churchill Livingstone.

The Toys (Safety) Regulations 1995 (SI 1995 No. 204) London: HMSO.

'Wired for Health: eczema in schools a guide for teachers' [online] available at www.eczema.org/school.htm [accessed 01/11/05].

Index

Acquired Immune Deficiency
    Syndrome 100
administration of medication 85–6
adrenaline medication 66
AIDS 100
allergies
    anaphylaxis 66–7
    asthma and 65
    food 65
    latex 20
    scope 64–5
anaphylaxis 66–7
animals 35
    campylobacter 35, 62
    salmonella 62
antibodies 6
aprons 19
aspirin 78, 87
asthma 67–70
    allergies and 65
athlete's foot 104

babies 6, 9
    food handling for 29, 59
baby rooms 14–15, 39
    equipment 25–6, 40–2, 54
    exclusions 45
    first aid 45–6
    health and safety 44–5
    hydration and nutrition 43
    minimum standards 40
    physical complaints 46–55
    sleeping 42–3, 53–4
baby walkers 42
bacteria 3–5 *see also individual terms*

ball pools 33
bedding 27, 40–1, 42
    on cot death 54
bleach 26
blinds 28
blockages 47
blood 31
body fluids 15, 19
    spillages 30–1
bottles 25–6, 41
breathing difficulties
    asthma 67–70
    croup 48
    epiglottitis 95–6

campylobacter 35, 62
carpets 14, 27, 28
chain of infection 3–5
chairs, high 28, 42
chewing, at teething 52
chickenpox 94 *see also* shingles
Children Act 1989 9
cleaning 14, 22, 23, 24, 26–7 *see also
    individual terms*
clothing 19–20, 31, 32
cold sterilisation 25
colds 16, 47–8
colic 46–7
confidentiality 89
conjunctivitis 94–5
Consultants in Communicable
    Diseases 97, 101, 102
Control of Substances Hazardous to
    Health Regulations 2004 (COSHH)
    13, 31, 87

convulsions 49–50
cot death 52–5
cots 40, 42, 54
coughs 48
  whooping 103
Coxsackie virus 96
cradle cap 48
creams
  barrier 29, 51
  for eczema 73–4
  for nappy rash 51
cross-contamination 61
croup 48
curtains 28

diabetes 70–2
diarrhoea 33, 35, 49, 62, 95 *see also*
  faeces
diphtheria 7, 101
dirt 22–3, 24
disinfection 23, 24–6, 31, 41
disposal of medication 88
drink 43, 60
  for diarrhoea and vomit 49
dust 24
duty of care 36

E. coli 63
ear infections 49
eczema 72–5
EHOs 61
emergencies viii, 88
  allergies 64, 65, 66–7
  asthma 69
  diphtheria 101
  epiglottitis 95–6
  epilepsy 77–8
  meningitis 97–8
  poisoning 52, 61–4
  poliomyelitis 102
environment 13, 14 *see also individual
  terms*
Environmental Health Officers 61
epiglottitis 95–6
epilepsy 75–8
Escherichia coli 63
exclusions 5, 45, 93

faeces 31, 35 *see also* diarrhoea

fever fits 49–50
fifth disease 96
first aid 45–6, 60
floors 27, 28
food 43
  allergies 65
  for diabetes 71
  for eczema 75
food handlers, clothing 20
food handling 29, 57–60
food poisoning
  campylobacter 62
  E. coli 63
  listeria 63–4
  risk factors 61–2
  salmonella 62–3
food service practices 57–60
  preparation areas 58
  preparing food 59
  utensils 59
fungal infections
  athlete's foot 104
  ringworm 105
  furniture 28

gels, for teething 52
German measles 7, 98–9 *see also*
  measles
gloves 19–20
glucose 70

hair
  care 9
  lice 104–5
hand, foot and mouth disease 96
hands, washing ix, 5, 13, 16–19, 58
hard surface toys 34–5
harnesses 42
hazards 13, 31, 44, 52
Health and Safety at Work etc. Act
  1974 13
healthcare plan 64, 81, 83, 84
health record 5, 83
heat infection 24–5
hepatitis A 101
hepatitis B 101–2
herpes zoster 99 *see also* chickenpox
Hib vaccination 7
HIV 100

hospitals
    appointments 81
    emergencies 88
Human Immunodeficiency Virus 100
hydration 43, 60
    for diarrhoea and vomit 49
hygiene 3 *see also individual terms*
hyperglycaemic reaction 72
hypochlorite 26
hypoglycaemic reaction 71–2

immunisation 5, 6–7, 11
immunity 5–6
impetigo 105
incubation signs 93
inhalers 68–70
insects 36
    head lice 104–5
insulin 70
insulin medication 70–1
itching
    from eczema 73–4
    from scabies 105–6

jaundice 101–2
jewellery 19

kitchens
    equipment 58, 59, 60
    first aid 60
    health and safety 58–9

larynx
    croup 48
    epiglottitis 95–6
latex gloves 19–20
laundry 31–2
lice 104–5
listeria 63–4

mats
    nappy changing 27, 29, 30
    sleeping 27
mattresses 40–1
measles 7, 97 *see also* German measles
measles, mumps, rubella vaccination 7
medication 81–9
MenC vaccination 7
meningitis 7, 50, 97–8

meningococcal C vaccination 7
microbes 3–5 *see also individual terms*
microwave 25, 41
milk 43
Milton cold sterilisation 25
mites 105–6
MMR vaccination 7
mumps 7, 98

nappies 29, 32, 51
nappy changing areas 28–30
nappy changing mats 27, 29, 30
nappy rash 50–2
nits 104–5
non-prescription medication 86–7
notifiable diseases
    diphtheria 101
    hepatitis A 101
    hepatitis B 101–2
    meningitis 97–8
    poliomyelitis 102
    tuberculosis 102
nutrition *see* food

ointments, for nappy rash 51
oral hygiene 8–9
outbreaks 14, 61–2

painkillers 78, 87
parasites
    lice 104–5
    mites 105–6
    worms 106
parents
    about epilepsy 78
    about medication 82
parvovirus 96
personal hygiene ix, 5, 9, 11, 13, 16–19,
    27, 58
pertussis 7, 103
pests 35–6
play equipment 33–4
playdough 33
poisoning 52
    food 61–4
policies 81 *see also individual terms*
poliomyelitis 7, 102
potties 30
pre-existing conditions 8

pregnancy
   chickenpox on 94
   German measles on 99
primary vaccination schedule 6

qualifications 9

rashes
   chickenpox 94
   German measles 7, 98–9
   hand, foot and mouth disease 96
   measles 7, 97
   meningitis 7, 50, 97–8
   nappy rash 50–2
   shingles 99
   slapped cheek syndrome 96
record keeping 5, 64, 81, 82–6, 89
refusals of medication 86
Reporting of Injuries, Diseases and
   Dangerous Occurrences Regulations
   1995 10, 87
Reye's syndrome 78
RIDDOR 10, 87
ringworm 105
rotavirus 33
rubbish 36–7
rubella 7, 98–9 see also measles

safety harnesses 42
safety management 87
salmonella 62–3
scabies 105–6
scratching
   from eczema 73–4
   from scabies 105–6
seizures
   epilepsy 75–8
   febrile 49–50
   generalised 75
self-management of medication 85–6
shingles 99 see also chickenpox
SIDS 52–5
slapped cheek syndrome 96
sleeping 42–3
   cot death 52–5

sleeping mats 27
smoking, on cot death 54
soft furnishings 28
soft toys 35
space allocation 15
spillages 30–1
staff 10 see also individual terms
sterilisation 25–6, 41
sticky eye 94–5
storage of medication management
   87–8
Sudden Infant Death Syndrome
   (SIDS) 52–5
supervision ratios 9–10
susceptibility 8
symbiosis 3

tables 28
TB 102
teeth 8–9
teething 41, 52
tetanus 7
toilets 13, 30
toys 27, 33, 34–5
training 9, 10, 57, 88–9
tuberculosis 102
tumbler test x, 50, 98

uniforms 32
upholstered furniture 28
urine 31, 70
utensils 59, 60

vaccination 5, 6–7, 11
vaccines 6–7
verrucas 106
vomit 31, 33, 49, 95

walkers 42
warts, verrucas 106
washing machines 32
waste bins 37
water 60
whooping cough 7, 103
worms 106